Dictionary of
Needlepoint
STITCHES

Dictionary of Needlepoint STITCHES

Ann E. Pester

Golden Press • New York
Western Publishing Company, Inc.
Racine, Wisconsin

diagrams by Liz Green

COVER PHOTOS: Doug Mellor

Library of Congress Catalog Card Number: 77–90089

Contents

Introduction

INTRODUCTION

"Needlepoint," as the term is commonly used, is the everyday name for the art of stitching a design with needle and yarn on special cotton canvas. More correctly, this type of stitchery is called canvas work (needlepoint is really a type of needle-made lace)—but, by any name, canvas work or needlepoint is embroidery, usually worked in wool yarn on an evenly woven, stiffened cotton material called canvas.

Needlepointing has been practiced in most civilized countries in some form since antiquity—and it remains, today, one of the most popular and creative of all hand arts.

In traditional needlepoint, the stitches cover the entire surface of the canvas, making a smooth, hard-wearing fabric that resembles hand-woven tapestry. Because of their firm construction, traditional needlepoint canvases make excellent covers for footstools, chairs, and pillows. Other favorites of needlepointers are wall hangings, rugs, pictures, and bell pulls—the pieces often inspired by old needlepoint hangings once used on drafty castle walls to help insulate the large rooms. Handbags, vests, belts, and small accessories are also popular items.

Another characteristic of traditional needlepoint is that it is worked exclusively in the basic Tent stitch, relying on design and color for its charm. Today, however, needlepoint has expanded beyond the traditional to include a variety of innovative stitches and creative design techniques that you can use to achieve new and interesting effects.

By working a design in a variety of stitches, you can give your canvas additional texture and special accents—making the design come "alive" in a way not possible with traditional needlepoint alone. You can use these plain and fancy variety stitches in combination with (or instead of) the traditional Tent stitch to give a "new" look to your needlepoint . . . to create original, one-of-a-kind designs . . . or to achieve special effects and textures—and your own personal stamp—on predesigned commercial canvases.

The creative challenge today lies in choosing the most effective stitches and combinations, for there are literally hundreds to intrigue the intrepid needlepointer. With the wealth of stitches to choose from in this book, you can make your needlepoint more dramatic—and more fun to work. And perhaps most satisfying of all, you can make your needlepoint uniquely and individually *yours*.

Especially today, needlepoint is an exciting, expressive art—a joy to stitch and a pleasure to behold!

HOW TO USE THIS BOOK

Following the Introduction is the *Detail List* (page 11), a chart that gives the basic Tent and all variety stitches in alphabetical order and catalogues what the stitches are best and most frequently used for (background, accent, special effects, and so on). Directions for using mono and penelope canvas (page 21) and the three basic methods of working the Tent stitch (page 27) follow.

The Tent stitch is the basis of all needlepoint. If you are a beginner, you should learn to work this stitch with ease before attempting the variety stitches. If you are an experienced needlepointer, you may wish to refresh your memory by reviewing the instructions and diagrams. With the Tent stitch mastered, you are ready to increase your repertoire of needlepoint stitches.

The section on *Variety Stitches* (page 31) gives directions with diagrams and Stitch Guides for working each of the stitches included in the Detail List. The advantages, disadvantages, main uses, and features of each stitch are discussed as well. Many stitches can be worked in several ways. The methods I have chosen to diagram are those that I have found the easiest to work, or those that give the fullest or most even coverage on both the back and front of the canvas.

The best way to learn any stitch is to have yarn, needle, and canvas in hand as you carefully read the directions and follow the diagrams and Stitch Guides. It's a good idea to practice a new stitch by working a small area with it—until you get the rhythm of the stitch—before you use it in your needlepoint design. I recommend that you try working up samples first, using four or five stitches at a time—you'll see how the stitches you've chosen actually look, how your yarn fills the canvas, and so on. Often your samples will be pretty enough to frame, and can serve as a record of the stitches you've tried.

Some hints on selecting variety stitches are given on page 32, and with the Detail List on page 12. Pick and choose among the stitches that appeal to you—or consult the Detail List to find a stitch to serve a particular purpose. You're sure to discover many special favorites.

There are separate sections detailing stitch combinations that work especially well as *Grounding Stitches* (page 155) and *Border Stitches* (page 165), although most variety stitches may be used for either of these purposes. Again, each stitch is accompanied by directions and diagrams.

General, practical advice for actually doing needlepoint (from tips on the fullness of the yarn to incorporating beads and "found" objects in your work) are discussed in the *Know-How Notes* (page 173)—the tricks of the trade that make needlepoint easy and pretty.

If a term is unfamiliar to you, check the *Glossary*, page 183, for a definition. If you can't find a stitch under the name you're familiar with, check the *Index to Stitches* (page 189)—for easy reference, I've tried to include most of the various names that stitches are known by. A *Bibliography* on page 188 lists interesting and useful books for further reading.

If you are a left-handed needlepointer, you have not been forgotten. Directions for *Working Left-handed* so that your stitches will slant in the same direction as right-handers' are given on pages 180 to 181.

Finally, in presenting this book, I want to extend my sincere thanks and appreciation to my mother, who has always given me her wholehearted encouragement for every project; to the late Kathryn Campbell Mock, who encouraged me to write the book and helped me get it started; to Ann Craven, who has given generously of her time and expertise to read the text and check diagrams; and to Caroline Greenberg, my understanding and patient editor.

Happy stitching to all!

Detail List

DETAIL LIST

The chart that follows on pages 14 to 19 provides a quick reference to the best uses for each stitch. Refer to it when you are looking for a stitch to fill a special need—or to see if a stitch is suitable for the purpose you have in mind.

The stitches are listed alphabetically, with "families" of stitches grouped together—for instance, Cross stitches, Gobelin stitches, and so forth. (If a stitch isn't listed under the name you're familiar with, check the Index to Stitches on page 189.)

The first column on the chart indicates the type of stitch, keyed as follows:

*Type   **A** Flat stitches (slanted, upright, horizontal)

B Cross stitches

C Knotted or tied-down stitches

D Combination stitches (made up of two or more stitches)

E Tufted stitches

F Trammed stitches

A check [X] in the **Background** column means a stitch may be used to fill in the area surrounding the central design and/or pattern motifs. **Utility** stitches are durable, and suitable for pieces that will receive hard wear. **Filling** stitches may be used for the design area, or any smaller area within a design.

Stitches checked in the fifth column are good for **Detail** —any small, important section in a design, or a special area such as eyes, flower centers, or outlines. Stitches suitable for **Accent Texture or Motif** give a definite accenting texture when they're used in groups or as an overall repeat. Some of the larger ones can also be used alone, as single motifs.

Two or More Colors of yarn can be used in working some stitches, and these are checked in the seventh column. To find a stitch that may be worked in several shades to give a dimensional effect, consult the eighth column—**Shading.** The **Special Effects** column includes bulky textures, eyelet stitches, tufting, and stitches that are excellent for stripes. Stitches checked under **Over-stitching** may also be worked on top of *finished* needlepoint to create special textures and accents. Very firm or extra strong stitches, suggested for needlepoint rugs, are checked in the **Rug Stitches** column.

Most stitches can be worked on either mono or penelope canvas, but the stitches indicated under the **Penelope Canvas** heading can be worked properly *only* on penelope canvas. Checks in the next two columns will tell you whether a stitch works up **Fast** or **Slow.** The last column gives the **Page Number** on which you'll find additional information, as well as the instructions and diagrams for working the stitch.

Note: Many stitches are checked in several columns because they are adaptable to a variety of uses. Others are less versatile. For instance, purely decorative stitches, which may snag, are generally not recommended for backgrounds on pieces that will receive hard wear. Keep in mind, however, that this chart indicates the best (or most common) uses for these stitches—not their *only* uses. Creative stitching methods and new uses are being devised all the time—you may develop a few yourself!

Stitch	*Type	Background	Utility	Filling	Detail	Two or More Colors	Accent Texture or Motif	Shading	Special Effects	Over-stitching	Rug Stitches	Penelope Canvas (ONLY)	Works FAST	Works SLOW	Page Number
Basic Tent Stitch															
CONTINENTAL	A	X	X	X	X	X		X	X		X		X		28
DIAGONAL TENT OR BASKET WEAVE	A	X	X	X				X	X		X		X		29
HALF CROSS	A	X	X	X	X	X		X	X		X	X	X		30
Variety Stitches															
ALGERIAN EYE	A				X		X		X	X				X	32
ALGERIAN PLAITED	B				X		X		X				X		33
BACK	A				X	X				X			X		34
BOKHARA COUCHING	F			X				X					X		34
BOX	A			X		X	X		X					X	35
BRAIDED	D						X		X				X		36
BRICK I	A	X	X	X		X	X	X					X		37
BRICK II	A	X	X	X		X	X	X					X		38
BUTTONHOLE, CLOSED	A			X	X	X			X	X			X		39
BYZANTINE	A	X		X		X		X					X		40
CASHMERE, DIAGONAL	A	X	X	X	X	X		X					X		41
CASHMERE, HORIZONTAL	A	X	X	X	X	X		X					X		42
CHAIN	D			X	X	X			X	X				X	43
CROSS STITCHES															
Closed Cross	B			X	X	X			X				X		44
Cross	B	X	X	X	X	X	X	X	X		X		X		44
Crossed Corners	B	X	X	X	X	X	X	X		X		X		X	46
Diagonal Cross	B	X		X		X	X		X					X	47
Double	B	X	X	X				X					X		48
Double Straight Cross	B	X		X		X	X		X				X		48
Large and Straight Cross	B	X		X		X			X					X	49

*See key on page 12

	Background *Type	Utility	Filling	Accent Texture or Motif / Detail	Two or More Colors	Shading	Special Effects	Over-stitching	Rug Stitches	Penelope Canvas (ONLY)	Works FAST	Works SLOW	Page Number
Long-Armed Cross	B	X	X		X			X		X	X		50
Long Cross	B		X	X	X			X				X	50
Long-Legged Cross	B	X	X		X			X		X	X		51
Montenegrin Cross	B	X	X	X	X			X		X	X		51
Oblong Cross	B	X		X	X				X		X		52
Oblong Cross with Back	B	X		X	X	X			X		X		52
Reversed Cross	B	X		X			X	X				X	53
St. George and St. Andrew Cross	B	X		X			X	X				X	53
Slanting Cross	B	X		X	X	X		X			X		54
Smyrna Cross	B	X		X	X	X		X	X		X		54
Squared-Off Cross	B	X			X	X		X				X	55
Tied-Down Cross	B			X	X	X		X	X			X	56
Trammed Cross	B	X	X	X	X	X	X					X	57
Triple Cross	B				X	X		X				X	58
Two-Sided Cross	B	X		X				X				X	59
Two-Sided Italian Cross	B	X		X	X						X		60
Upright Cross	B	X	X	X	X	X	X	X			X		61
DAMASK	A	X		X				X			X		61
DARNING	A	X	X	X			X	X		X		X	62
DIAMOND EYELET	A			X	X			X				X	64
DOUBLE BASKET WEAVE	A	X	X	X				X	X		X		65
DOUBLE SATIN STAR	D	X			X	X						X	66
EASTERN	D			X				X	X	X		X	68
ENCROACHING OBLIQUE	A	X		X			X				X		69
EYE	A	X		X	X			X				X	70
FEATHER	F			X	X	X		X				X	72

*See key on page 12

	Background *Type	Utility	Filling	Detail	Two or More Colors	Accent Texture or Motif	Shading	Special Effects	Over-stitching	Rug Stitches	Penelope Canvas (ONLY)	Works FAST	Works SLOW	Page Number
FERN	A		X	X		X			X			X		74
FISHBONE	B	X		X		X			X			X		74
FLORENCE	A	X	X	X					X			X		75
FLORENTINE EMBROIDERY														
Bargello	A	X	X	X					X			X		76
Florentine	A	X		X					X			X		79
Hungarian	A	X	X	X					X			X		80
Hungarian Ground	A	X	X	X			X					X		80
Old Florentine	A	X		X			X					X		82
FLOWER	D				X	X		X					X	83
FLY	C	X	X	X		X			X	X		X		84
FRENCH	C	X	X	X					X		X	X		84
FRENCH KNOT	D				X	X		X	X				X	85
FRINGE	E							X	X			X		86
GOBELIN STITCHES														
Encroaching Gobelin	A	X	X	X					X			X		88
Plaited Gobelin	A	X	X	X					X			X		88
Slanting Gobelin	A	X	X	X	X				X			X		89
Straight Gobelin	A	X	X	X	X				X			X		89
Upright Gobelin	A	X	X	X	X				X			X		90
Upright Split Gobelin	A	X		X	X				X	X		X		90
Wide Gobelin	A	X		X					X			X		91
GREEK	B	X	X	X		X			X		X	X		91
HERRINGBONE STITCHES														
Continental Herringbone	A	X	X	X	X				X		X	X		92
Herringbone Couching	D			X		X	X		X			X		93

*See key on page 12

	Background *Type	Utility	Filling	Detail	Accent Texture or Motif	Two or More Colors	Shading	Special Effects	Over-stitching	Rug Stitches	Penelope Canvas (ONLY)	Works FAST	Works SLOW	Page Number
Herringbone I	B	X		X					X		X		X	94
Herringbone II	B	X		X					X				X	95
Two-Color Herringbone	B			X		X	X		X				X	96
Wide Stripe Herringbone	B	X					X		X				X	97
JACQUARD	A	X	X	X		X	X						X	98
KALEM	A	X	X	X	X		X		X		X		X	99
KNIT	A	X	X	X		X	X						X	99
KNIT-ON-THE-DIAGONAL	A			X	X		X		X				X	100
KNITTING	A	X	X	X							X	X		100
KNOTTED	C	X	X	X				X			X		X	101
LEAF	A	X		X			X		X	X	X		X	102
LEVIATHAN STITCHES														
Double Leviathan	B			X	X	X		X	X				X	104
Triple Leviathan	D			X	X	X		X	X				X	105
MILANESE	A	X		X		X	X						X	106
MOSAIC STITCHES														
Diagonal Mosaic	A	X	X	X	X	X	X	X					X	108
Horizontal Mosaic	A	X	X	X	X	X	X	X					X	109
Hungarian Mosaic	A			X			X	X	X				X	110
Reverse Mosaic	A	X	X	X		X	X						X	110
NORWICH	D	X					X	X	X				X	111
ORIENTAL	A	X		X			X						X	112
PARISIAN	A	X	X	X			X	X					X	114
PLAIT	B	X		X		X			X				X	115
PLAITED	B			X		X	X						X	116
PLAITED EDGING	B									X	X		X	117

*See key on page 12

	Background *Type	Utility	Filling	Detail	Accent Texture or Motif	Two or More Colors	Shading	Special Effects	Over-stitching	Rug Stitches	Penelope Canvas (ONLY)	Works FAST	Works SLOW	Page Number
RAY	A	X		X		X	X		X	X			X	118
RENAISSANCE	D	X	X	X					X				X	119
REP	A	X	X	X	X							X	X	120
REVERSED EYELET	A	X				X	X		X				X	121
REVERSED HALF CROSS	A	X	X	X	X		X				X	X	X	122
ROCOCO I	C			X					X				X	122
ROCOCO II	C	X	X	X		X			X				X	124
ROMAN	C	X	X	X		X			X	X			X	125
ROUMANIAN COUCHING	F	X		X					X				X	126
SATIN STITCHES														
Mosaic Diamond	A	X		X		X	X	X	X				X	127
Mosaic Star	D	X		X		X	X		X				X	128
Satin	A	X		X	X				X				X	129
Satin Herringbone	A	X		X				X	X				X	129
Satin Motif	A	X				X	X						X	130
SCOTCH STITCHES														
Chequer	A	X		X		X	X		X				X	131
Diagonal	A	X		X			X						X	132
Flat	A	X		X		X	X						X	133
Flat Diagonal	A	X		X		X	X						X	134
Moorish	A	X		X					X				X	135
Scotch	A	X		X		X		X	X				X	135
Scottish	A	X		X		X	X						X	136
Woven	A	X		X		X	X							137
												X		
SHEAF	C			X		X			X	X			X	137
SHELL	D			X			X		X				X	138

*See key on page 12

	Background *Type	Utility	Filling	Detail	Accent Texture or Motif	Two or More Colors	Shading	Special Effects	Over-stitching	Rug Stitches	Penelope Canvas (ONLY)	Works FAST	Works SLOW	Page Number
SLAV STITCHES														
Oblique Slav, Diagonal	A	X		X					X			X		140
Oblique Slav, Horizontal	A	X		X					X			X		141
STAR	A	X	X	X	X	X							X	142
STEM	A	X	X	X			X	X				X		142
TRAMÉ STITCHES														
Split Tramé	F	X		X					X				X	143
Tramé	F	X	X	X					X				X	144
Vertical Tramé	F	X		X					X	X			X	145
TRIANGLE	D	X					X	X	X			X		145
TUFTED STITCHES														
Double Knotted	E			X	X			X		X			X	146
Plush	E	X	X	X	X	X	X		X	X		X		147
Single Knotted	E	X	X	X	X	X	X	X	X	X	X	X		148
Surrey	E	X	X	X	X	X	X	X	X	X	X	X		149
Velvet	E	X	X	X	X	X	X		X				X	150
VAN DYKE	B			X		X			X			X		151
WEB	D	X	X	X			X	X	X				X	152
ZIGZAG	A	X		X			X	X	X			X		154

*See key on page 12

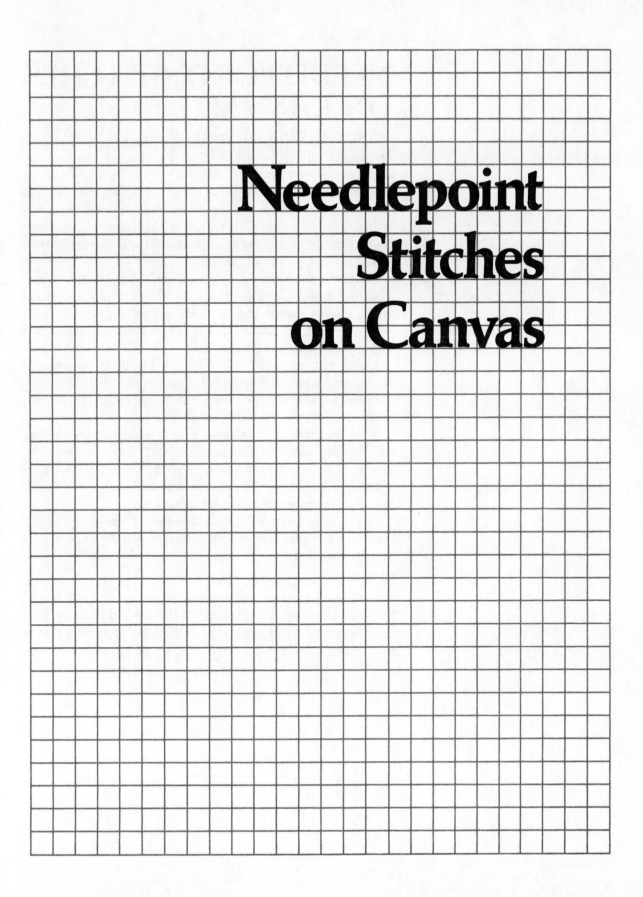

Needlepoint Stitches on Canvas

NEEDLEPOINT STITCHES ON CANVAS

MONO CANVAS (single thread canvas)

This canvas has an even, open weave and is easy to work on. On mono canvas, 1 horizontal and 1 vertical thread form each intersection. As you will note on the diagram, the threads cross each other in an over-under manner and are not interlocked. Every other vertical thread is "held down" by a horizontal thread that crosses it, and every other horizontal thread is held down by a vertical thread.

Another kind of mono canvas, called interlocking, is also available. Interlocking (or leno) is similar to the traditional mono canvas except that it does not have an over-under weave; instead, the single threads, which are 2-ply, are locked together and cannot be separated.

Mono and interlocking canvas are available in different widths and sizes. The size of the canvas is indicated by the number of threads to the running inch. For instance, 10 count canvas has 10 threads to the inch.

Both these mono canvases are evenly woven, so the stitches will be even whether the canvas is held vertically (with the selvage at the side) or horizontally (with the selvage at top or bottom). But take care: Don't turn the canvas after stitching is begun or your stitches will slant incorrectly.

Single thread canvas and double thread canvas (page 24) can be used interchangeably unless directions specify one kind or the other.

Note: In working certain variety stitches on mono canvas, it is sometimes helpful to put the needle under a "held-down" thread. The reason for this is that otherwise, if the yarn isn't full enough or if the stitch is pulled too tight, the stitch may slip through to the next mesh. (Yarn will not slip on interlocking or on double thread canvas.)

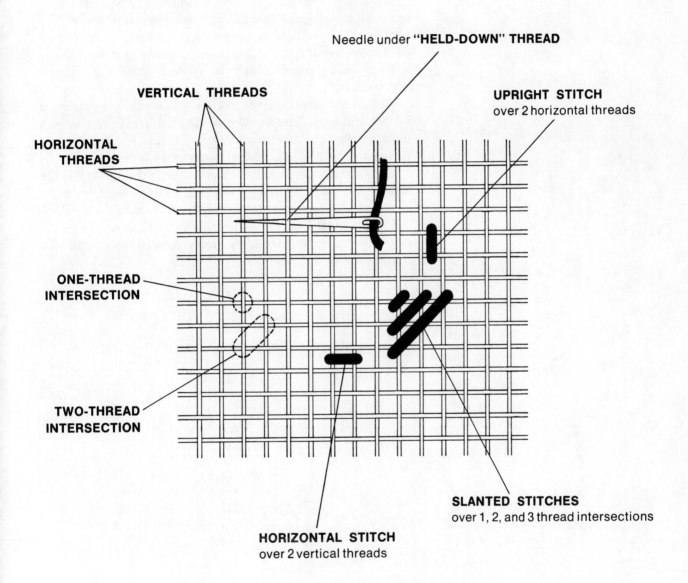

Needle under **"HELD-DOWN" THREAD**

VERTICAL THREADS

UPRIGHT STITCH
over 2 horizontal threads

HORIZONTAL THREADS

ONE-THREAD INTERSECTION

TWO-THREAD INTERSECTION

SLANTED STITCHES
over 1, 2, and 3 thread intersections

HORIZONTAL STITCH
over 2 vertical threads

PENELOPE CANVAS (double thread or duo canvas)

This canvas is woven with 2 warp threads and 2 filling threads forming each intersection. The double threads on penelope canvas make it possible to work both Petit Point (very small stitches) and regular needlepoint on the same piece. For regular needlepoint, each double thread is worked as one; for Petit Point, the double threads are separated (see diagram) and a Tent (Continental) stitch is worked over each single intersection.

Like mono canvas, penelope canvas is available in different widths and sizes. The number of double threads to the inch indicates the size of the canvas. For instance, 10 count penelope canvas has 10 double threads to the inch.

Penelope canvas should be worked with the selvage at the side of the piece. (If the selvage has been cut off, hold the canvas so that the most closely paired threads run vertically.)

Double thread canvas and single thread canvas (page 22) can be used interchangeably unless directions specifically require one or the other.

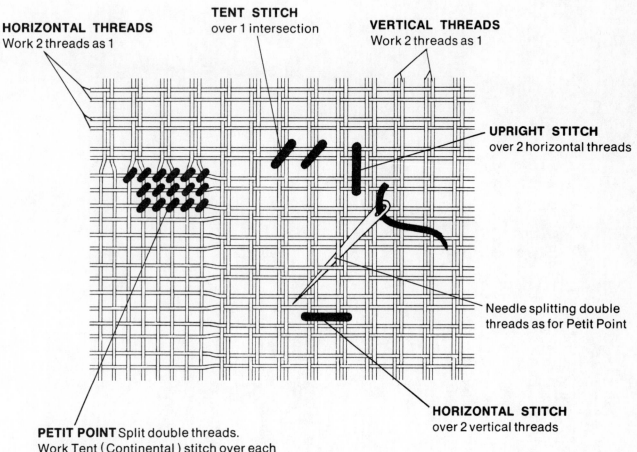

HORIZONTAL THREADS
Work 2 threads as 1

TENT STITCH
over 1 intersection

VERTICAL THREADS
Work 2 threads as 1

UPRIGHT STITCH
over 2 horizontal threads

Needle splitting double
threads as for Petit Point

PETIT POINT Split double threads.
Work Tent (Continental) stitch over each
intersection. Make four stitches in
same area as one "regular" stitch.

HORIZONTAL STITCH
over 2 vertical threads

Basic Tent Stitch

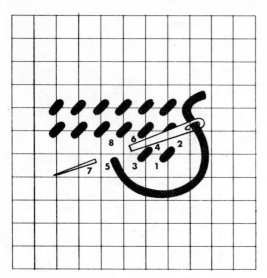

BASIC TENT STITCH

Tent stitch is the primary stitch used for all needlepoint. It is a small stitch worked over 1 thread intersection on mono canvas or 1 double thread intersection on penelope canvas. It is always slanted from left to right. Tent stitch can be worked by three different methods: the Continental stitch (below), the Diagonal Tent or Basket Weave stitch (facing page), and the Half Cross stitch (page 30).

CONTINENTAL STITCH (called Petit Point when worked on high count canvas or linen; see note below)

The Tent stitch, the basic needlepoint stitch, is most often worked by this method. The stitch is small, slanting up diagonally from left to right over the intersection of 1 vertical and horizontal thread of the canvas, making a firm, even, hard-wearing surface. This form of the basic Tent stitch completely covers the back of the canvas with even, slanting stitches. Many needlepointers use only this stitch. Works fast.

Continental stitch, as well as all other needlepoint stitches, should be worked with a yarn just full enough to fit the canvas. For example, when using 3-ply Persian wool, use one full 3-ply strand on 10 mesh canvas, use a 2-ply strand on 12 or 14 mesh canvas, and use a 1-ply strand on 18 mesh canvas. To work 1 square inch on 10 mesh canvas, approximately 1¼ yards of 3-ply yarn is required. A smaller mesh (higher count) uses just a bit more wool.

Work Continental stitch in rows across the canvas, starting at the upper right edge of the area to be covered. Turn the canvas around to stitch the next row, always working from right to left.

The canvas will pull crooked as it is worked, but this isn't permanent. The canvas can be blocked out to its original shape when the needlepoint is finished.

Variation: Work in vertical rows from top to bottom. This method is good for detail, outlining, initials, and so on.

Note: Petit Point is the term used for needlepoint stitches that are very small. When the Continental stitch is worked on 18, 22, 24, or higher count mono or interlocking canvas — or on 10, 12, or 14 mesh penelope canvas — it is called Petit Point. To work Petit Point on penelope canvas, each pair of threads, both vertical and horizontal, must be picked open with the needle, and a small Continental stitch worked over each intersection (see page 24).

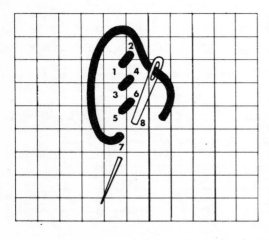

DIAGONAL TENT or BASKET WEAVE STITCH

In this method, the basic Tent stitch is worked on the diagonal. This is the best way to do the Tent stitch for large areas such as backgrounds. On the front of the canvas each stitch slants up from left to right over 1 thread intersection. This is a hard-wearing utility stitch that gives good back padding, and it does not pull the canvas out of shape. Works fast.

You will need about 1¼ yards of 3-ply Persian yarn to work 1 square inch on 10 mesh canvas.

Work in diagonal rows, starting at the upper right of the area to be covered. Work alternate rows from top to bottom, bottom to top — *do not turn work.* When working *up,* the needle is always *horizontal* under 2 threads at the back of the canvas (see first diagram). When working *down,* the needle is always *vertical* under 2 threads at the back.

Following the first diagram, work one stitch in the upper right corner of area. Work the second stitch to the left of the first stitch (like a Continental stitch); work the third stitch *below* the first stitch. These two stitches are the second, or *down,* row (shown as dark stitches on the diagram).

The third row begins immediately under the last stitch. Work *up* to the top edge (light stitches on the diagram), with the needle horizontal under 2 threads to make each stitch.

To keep edges straight, each row is one stitch longer than the last. After you've mastered this stitch for straight-edged areas like backgrounds, you'll find it's adaptable and easy to work in smaller irregular and design areas, too.

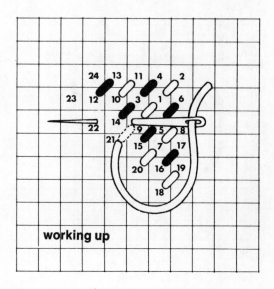

working up

Stitch Guide

	from	to
first stitch	1	2
down	3	4
	5	6
up	7	8
	9	1
	10	11
down	12	13
	14	3
	15	5
	16	17
up	18	19
	20	7
	21	9
	22	

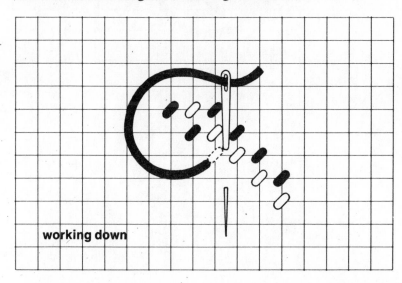

working down

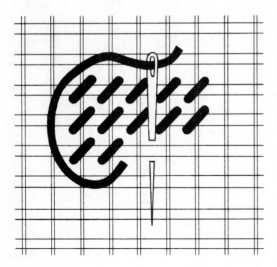

HALF CROSS STITCH

This version of the basic Tent stitch should be used *only* on penelope canvas. The front of the canvas looks the same as with the Continental and the Diagonal Tent or Basket Weave stitches, but the back has less coverage. This stitch does not pull the canvas out of shape. It works quickly and uses less yarn than the other versions of the basic Tent stitch.

One yard of 3-ply Persian yarn works about 1 square inch on 10 mesh canvas.

Starting at the top of the area to be covered, work in horizontal rows from left to right over 1 vertical and horizontal thread. (For regular needlepoint on penelope canvas, each pair of double canvas threads is usually referred to as 1 thread.) The needle is always vertical under 1 horizontal thread at the back of the canvas. Turn canvas to work the next row.

Variation: Work from the bottom to the top in vertical rows. The needle is always horizontal under 1 vertical thread at the back of the canvas. (Use only on penelope canvas.)

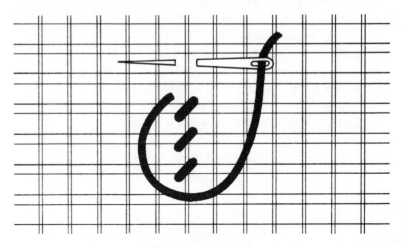

Variety Stitches

VARIETY STITCHES

The stitches that follow may be used to create original needlepoint designs, or to achieve special effects and textures—and your own personal stamp—on predesigned canvases.

There are dozens of general-use and utility stitches here (stitches that are particularly good to use when you're working on a piece that will receive a lot of wear), as well as a number of very decorative "fancy" stitches. There are stitches that can be used to create a central motif (with the background worked in Tent stitch—or perhaps in one of the other stitches recommended for backgrounds); stitches to use for allover repeat designs; stitches for accents and special effects; combination stitches (made up of two or more individual stitches used together to form still another stitch pattern); tufted stitches to use for lush pile effects; and many, many more.

The stitches are listed alphabetically, with "families" of stitches grouped together—for instance, Cross stitches, Gobelin stitches, Herringbone stitches, and so forth. (If you're not sure where to find a particular stitch, check the Index to Stitches on page 189.)

You may wish to jump right in and try a stitch that strikes your fancy—or consult the Detail List (page 11) to pick a stitch that serves a particular purpose. Most of the variety stitches are easy to work—even the ones that look complicated. To start, take your needle, yarn, and canvas in hand. Read the text carefully, and follow the diagram and Stitch Guide until you get the rhythm of the stitch. Practice before trying a new stitch on your needlepoint design.

Remember, when you're picking stitches to enhance your next piece of needlepoint, don't go overboard. Be selective. Not every stitch is for general use. The stitches you've chosen will be part of an overall design; they should complement each other and the entire piece in size, texture, and color. Too many stitches—or stitches ill-placed—and your needlepoint will be in danger of looking like a hodgepodge. Chosen well and executed carefully, variety stitches can add character and individuality to your work.

ALGERIAN EYE STITCH

This is a small stitch, best worked in diagonal rows if being used for a large area. It is similar to the Star stitch (page 142), except here the yarn covers every 2 threads twice to form alternating pairs of slanted and straight stitches. Be sure your wool is not too full — try 2 plies of Persian wool for 10 mesh canvas, or 1 ply for 12 or 14 count canvas. This is a decorative stitch that works slowly, and it's a yarn-eater, too!

Starting at lower left of unit, cover 2 threads twice for each pair of stitches (there are eight double stitches to a unit). Work from the outside of the unit *into* the center mesh. (For even, smooth work, the needle is always worked into the center mesh in eyelet stitches.) Complete each "eye" before going on to the next.

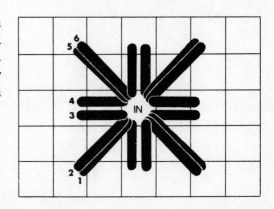

ALGERIAN PLAITED STITCH

This is a herringbone pattern stitch, similar to the Plait stitch (page 115). It is a general-use stitch that's also good for borders. It can be worked over from 3 to 6 horizontal threads and 2 vertical threads. Works fast.

Work in horizontal rows from left to right. At the back of the canvas the needle is *always* horizontal, inserted from right to left under 2 threads, first at bottom, then at top of row. This stitch *must* be worked from the left. At the end of each row, fasten off the yarn and start again at the left.

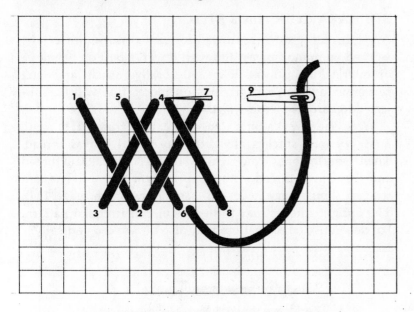

Stitch Guide

from	to
1	2
3	4
5	6
2	7
4	8
6	

BACK STITCH

A general-use stitch, the Back stitch is frequently used to fill bare spots, for accents, and for outlining an area. Vary yarn thickness and type as necessary for pattern. Works fast.

Work area from right to left over 1 or 2 vertical threads. (This stitch can also be worked from top to bottom over horizontal threads.)

Stitch Guide

from	to
1	2
3	1
4	3
5	

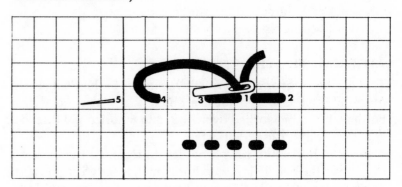

BASKET WEAVE STITCH (see Basic Tent Stitch, page 28)

BOKHARA COUCHING STITCH

An embroidery stitch borrowed for canvas work, this can be worked on mono canvas, although it works best on penelope or interlocking canvas. It is a decorative stitch, and isn't recommended for backgrounds on pieces that will be subjected to hard use. Works fast.

Work one row at a time across the canvas from left to right. First, lay long stitches along the horizontal canvas thread. Then, working back from right to left, tie down the laid thread and the canvas thread with small upright stitches. The laid stitches should vary in length (see Tramé stitch, page 144). The upright stitches may form a regular or irregular pattern. For decorative effect, pattern may also be worked vertically.

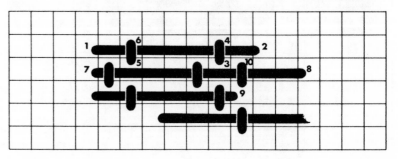

BOX STITCH (Perspective stitch, Reverse Slanting stitch)

A stitch for special effects, this is most effective when worked in two bold colors. It works slowly, and it's a yarn-eater, too!

Begin work at top of area and work rows of units across area from left to right. Each unit is made of four groups of three slanted stitches (each over 2 vertical and horizontal threads).

With first color, begin first unit with three slanting stitches *up to right.* Work the second group of three stitches slanting *up to left,* working into the same meshes as the first three stitches. Using a second color, work the third group of three stitches from mesh 7 (the same mesh the second group started in), slanting *down to left* and partially covering two stitches of the second group. Bring needle up in mesh 5 to begin the final three stitches. These slant *down to right* and partially cover two stitches of the first group. The complete unit covers 6 horizontal and 4 vertical threads.

Work units across the canvas in horizontal rows. The next row of units is worked below the row just completed. Start from the left and 2 threads to right of the first unit so units will alternate and encroach by 1 thread. (A half unit may be used to fill in the area at beginning and end of rows to keep edges even.)

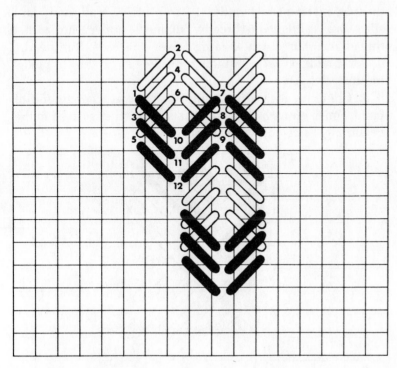

Stitch Guide

	from	to
first group	1	2
first color	3	4
	5	6
second group	7	2
first color	8	4
	9	6
third group	7	10
second color	8	11
	9	12
fourth group	5	12
second color	3	11
	1	10

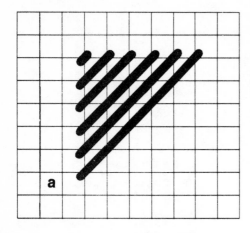

a

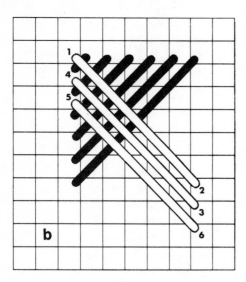

b

BRAIDED STITCH (Point de Tresse stitch, Ribbon stitch)

A complicated-looking stitch that is relatively easy to work, the Braided stitch makes a lovely banding, border, or edge for decorative pieces. On the front of the canvas it gives a puffy, braided look. On the back, there's very little coverage, so this isn't a stitch for hard wear. Works fast.

a. Work from top to bottom over 6 vertical threads. Begin with six foundation stitches slanting *up to right* over first 1, then 2, 3, 4, 5, and 6 thread intersections, covering the upper left corner of the 6 canvas threads that will be the foundation of your braid (follow diagram **a**). **Note:** If working on mono canvas, your Braid stitch will be more secure if the first vertical thread is a "held-down" thread (see page 22).

b. Bring the needle up in first mesh in upper left corner; slant stitch *down to right* over the first six stitches and 6 thread intersections. Insert needle under 1 horizontal thread and slant stitch *up to left* over 6 thread intersections. Put needle under 1 horizontal thread and slant stitch *down to right* over 6 thread intersections (see diagram **b**). Run needle under braid at back, bringing it up in same mesh as the last stitch of the six foundation stitches, mesh 7 (see diagram **c**).

c. Slant stitch *up to right* over 6 horizontal and vertical threads, insert needle under 1 horizontal thread, and slant stitch *down to left* over 6 threads. Put needle under 1 horizontal thread and slant stitch *up to right* over 6 threads. Run needle under braid at back, bringing needle up in mesh below mesh 5.

d. Continue alternating groups of three stitches to end of band. Finish off with graduated slanting stitches as used in the beginning. Fasten off yarn at back.

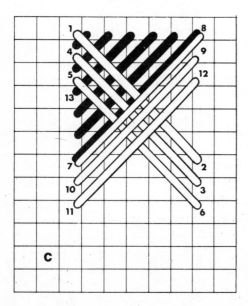

c

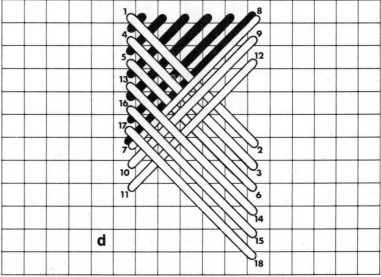

d

BRICK STITCH I (Alternating stitch)

An old favorite that is excellent for large areas, this stitch blends well with other stitches. (See also Upright Gobelin stitch, page 90.) It is a popular utility stitch that gives a firm backing. Wool must be full or canvas will show — try 4-ply yarn on 10 count canvas. Works quickly.

Work rows from left to right, then return right to left. The upright stitches (yarn positioned between vertical threads) may be over either 2 or 4 horizontal threads. Skip 1 mesh between each stitch. The return row fits into the first, with each upright stitch worked into the skipped mesh of the previous row.

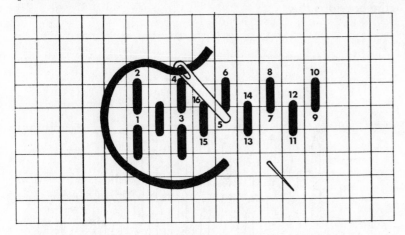

Variation: Double Brick. Same as above, except each stitch is doubled. Work two upright stitches, skip 2 meshes, work two stitches, and so on. Return row encroaches in same manner as above.

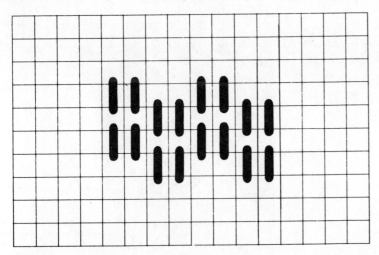

BRICK STITCH II (Irish stitch)

This looks like Brick stitch I on the front of the canvas, but uses less wool and does not cover the back so evenly. This is a general-use stitch that works quickly after a bit of practice.

Work upright stitches in rows over and back, starting at the left. Make first stitch *up* over 2 horizontal threads, bring needle up in next mesh below and to right, stitch *up* over 2 horizontal threads, bring needle up in next mesh below and to right, make stitch *down* over 2 horizontal threads, bring needle up in next mesh above and to right, stitch *up* over 2 threads, and so on to end of area to be covered. On return row, work stitches *up* and *down* following pattern and fitting stitches into the previous row.

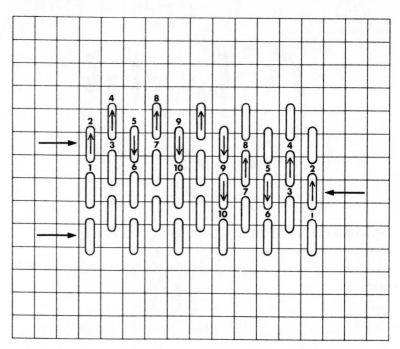

BUTTONHOLE STITCH, CLOSED

This is an embroidery stitch that adapts to canvas for decorative or special effects. It forms an upright stitch with a horizontal base. The wool must be full (as for all upright stitches) or the canvas will show. This stitch makes a firm, even back. It can also be worked over finished needlepoint. Works quickly.

Work in rows from right to left. Bring needle up in mesh at bottom of first row. Carry wool to left and hold with thumb. Working to the left, insert needle over 2 horizontal threads and between the next 2 vertical threads so it comes out in the next mesh to left of beginning. Point of needle is *over* the yarn held to the left, so that the yarn loops, making an L-shaped stitch. Continue. Hold yarn to left, insert needle vertically between next 2 threads and under 2 horizontal threads, looping yarn as needle is brought out. One thrust of the needle makes each stitch.

Work to end of row and fasten off. Start next row at the right and 2 threads below, and work in the same manner.

BYZANTINE STITCH

An old classic, this general-use stitch is excellent for covering large areas completely and rapidly. It's quick and easy to do. Be careful, though — don't pull stitches tight!

Work rows diagonally down from top left to bottom right, then up from bottom right to top left. Stitches are slanted up to the right, and may be worked over from 3 to 6 vertical and horizontal threads in even steps of four, five, or six stitches. (However, the longer the stitch, the less hard-wearing the surface.) By working the rows first from top to bottom and then from bottom to top (don't turn the canvas), the slant of the stitches on the back alternates, and the canvas doesn't pull so crooked.

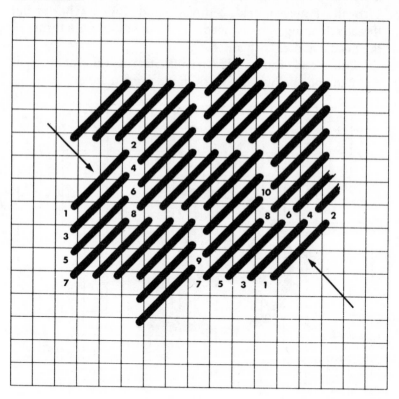

CASHMERE STITCH, DIAGONAL

This is a small, hard-wearing utility stitch that makes a fine-textured surface. The back is well covered, with stitch positions alternating, and the canvas does not pull out of shape so much. Works fast.

Work in diagonal rows. First work from upper left to lower right, then return from bottom right up to left. Each unit is composed of three stitches — slanted over 1 intersection, then over 2 intersections *twice*; repeat. The next row fits into the first, following pattern line.

Note: Light stitches on the diagram show partial pattern stitches needed to fill the area evenly. These fill-in stitches may be done after pattern area has been completed.

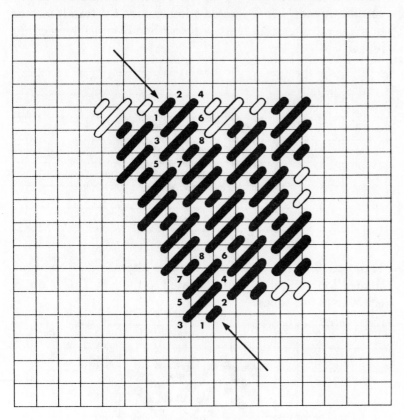

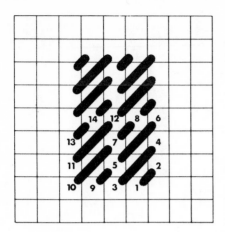

Stitch Guide

	from	to
first unit	1	2
	3	4
	5	6
	7	8
second unit	9	5
	10	7
	11	12
	13	14

CASHMERE STITCH, HORIZONTAL

Like the diagonal Cashmere stitch (page 41), this is a hard-wearing utility stitch. It can be most effective worked in two colors. The stitch makes a firm, even back. Works fast.

Units of four stitches each are worked in horizontal rows over 3 horizontal and 2 vertical threads. Using slanted stitches, work over 1 thread intersection, over 2 intersections *twice*, then over 1 intersection; repeat. Rows may be worked from left to right or from right to left. When working from right to left, each unit is worked from the bottom up (as diagrammed at left); when working from left to right, units are worked from top to bottom of row.

Variation A: Each unit is worked over 4 horizontal and 2 vertical threads. Work slanted stitches over 1 thread intersection, over 2 intersections *three times*, then over 1 intersection; repeat.

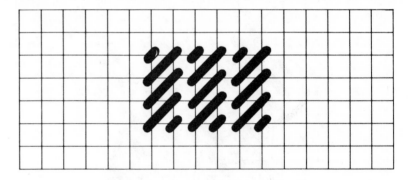

Variation B: The slant of the units is alternated — one unit slanted to the right, one unit slanted to the left. This is quite effective in two tones.

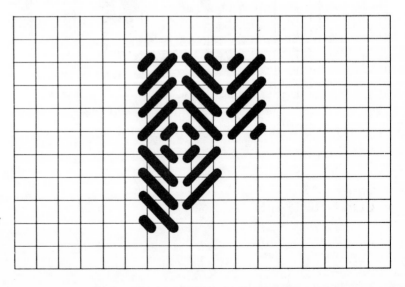

CHAIN STITCH

An embroidery stitch used for special effects on canvas, it is easiest to work this stitch on penelope canvas, though it can be worked on mono canvas if care is taken. Work over at least 2 canvas threads to make a firm stitch and prevent slipping. Adjust wool to proper thickness for desired effect. For example, on 10 count canvas, try a 2-ply strand. This is a decorative stitch that gives a firm backing. Works up rather slowly.

Vertical rows are worked from top to bottom of area. Bring needle up at 1 (see diagram), carry yarn down over 2 (or more) horizontal threads and, while holding yarn down with thumb, reinsert needle in first mesh and bring it out over the held yarn at 3. This makes a loop stitch on the surface. Each new stitch starts in the same mesh that the preceding stitch finished in.

Note: Long Chain stitches may be worked with Back stitches (page 34) inserted to cover the canvas, or Chain stitches can be worked over *finished* needlepoint to outline, or to give accent or dimensional bulk to an area.

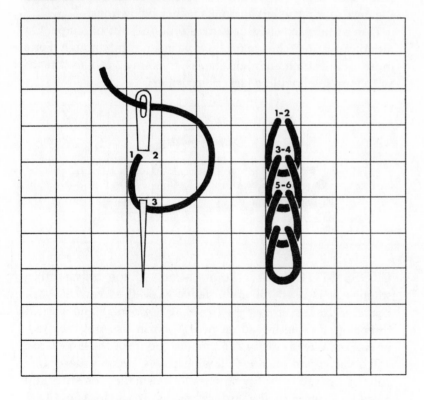

CONTINENTAL STITCH (see Basic Tent Stitch, page 28)

Cross Stitches

There are many varieties of the basic Cross stitch, but all have two or more slanted or straight stitches with the second (and succeeding) stitches crossing the first stitch. Generally, cross stitches make a firm, durable surface — unless they are used decoratively by working with long stitches to give a lacey or open effect.

CLOSED CROSS STITCH (Cat stitch, Catch stitch) — a small stitch that gives a herringbone effect. It covers the canvas well on the front but not on the back. This stitch is more decorative than utilitarian; it's excellent for ribbing or stripes. (See also Long Cross stitch, page 50.) Works fairly fast.

Each row is worked from left to right over 2 horizontal threads. Starting at the top left, slant stitch *down to right* over 2 horizontal and vertical threads, insert needle under 1 vertical thread, slant stitch *up to right* over 2 horizontal threads and 1 vertical thread, insert needle under 1 vertical thread, slant stitch *down to right* and continue to end. Fasten off yarn. Start the next row at the left again, 2 meshes below mesh 1.

Don't pull yarn tight or canvas will pull out of shape. On mono canvas, stitches may slip if yarn isn't full enough. For a more secure stitch on mono canvas, try using 2 canvas threads as 1. Your stitch will be larger but firmer.

Stitch Guide

from	to
1	2
3	4
5	6
2	7
4	8
6	9
7	

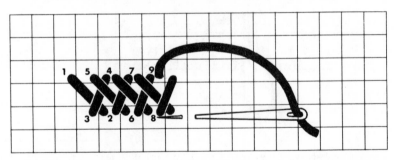

CROSS STITCH (Gros Point) — one of the oldest utility stitches. It is used for embroidery as well as canvas work. Usually crosses are worked over 2 horizontal and vertical threads (1 double thread on penelope canvas), but they may be worked over as many as 6 threads. (Some of the large Cross stitch variations on the following pages become decorative stitches instead of utility stitches.) The smaller the stitch, the more hard-wearing the surface. Adjust wool thickness to fit canvas as well as the size of the cross. Try 2-ply yarn for crosses over 2 threads on 10 or 12 count canvas, 1-ply on 14 count; 3-ply yarn for crosses over more than 2 threads. This stitch works fairly quickly after a bit of practice.

The basic Cross stitch may be worked in two ways:

On mono canvas, work horizontal rows from right to left, completing each cross before starting the next.

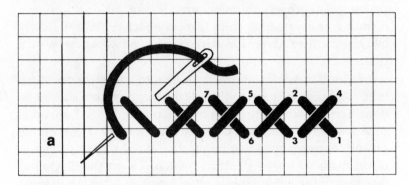

Stitch Guide

from	to
1	2
3	4
3	5
6	2
6	

On penelope canvas, begin working horizontal rows from the left. On the first journey, working from left to right, make half the cross (see Half Cross stitch, page 30). Then complete the cross on the return journey, working from right to left.

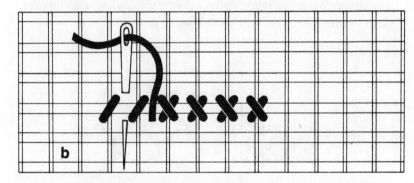

Crosses may be worked in diagonal rows, too. Work from bottom right to top left. (See diagram below.)

For a smooth, even look, be sure all top stitches of all crosses are slanted in the same direction.

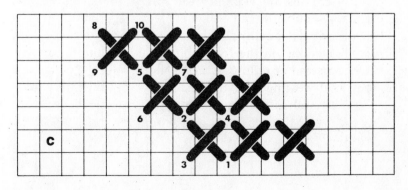

Stitch Guide

from	to
1	2
3	4
2	5
6	7
5	8
9	10
8	

CROSSED CORNERS STITCH (Rice stitch, William and Mary stitch) — a very old, small stitch that has always been popular with needlepointers. It is a utility as well as a decorative stitch, especially good for detailing, color blending, and special effects. A thick yarn is best for the large cross, but for crossing the corners a thinner yarn, often of silk or cotton, in a blending or contrasting color is most effective. Works slowly because the area covered is worked twice. (It works faster on a frame.)

Authorities differ somewhat on how to complete the stitch unit — though most agree that all the basic crosses should be done first over the entire area to be worked. Work horizontal rows from *right to left* (see Cross stitch, page 44). Then, on the second journey, again working from the right, cross each arm of the cross with a small slanted stitch. To get the rhythm of this part of the stitch takes a bit of practice — just remember that the needle is *always* vertical or horizontal at the back, making an even, regular backing. Follow diagram **a** and the Stitch Guide until you get the idea.

To work one complete unit at a time, with one continuous thread, see diagram **b** and follow the Stitch Guide. Work from right to left.

Stitch Guide

a. from	to
second journey 1	2
3	1
4	2
3	4
5	3
6	5
7	3
6	7
8	

b. from	to
1	2
3	4
5	6
7	5
8	6
7	8
3	

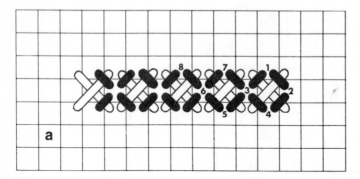

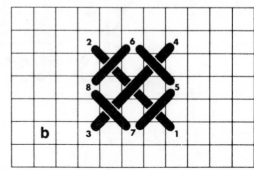

Variation: On larger units (over 4 or more threads), the arms of the basic cross may be crossed with two slanting stitches.

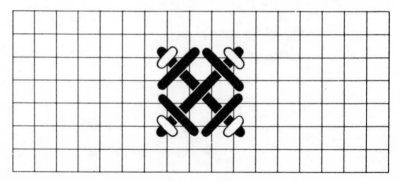

DIAGONAL CROSS STITCH — a novelty stitch worked in diagonal rows from bottom right to top left of area, usually over 4 threads. A decorative stitch that makes a nice texture, it covers canvas fairly well. Works slowly.

Three stitches make each cross-and-bar unit. Start with an upright stitch over 4 horizontal threads. Then, from the same mesh (1), slant stitch *up to right* over 2 vertical and horizontal threads. Bring needle up 4 meshes to the left and cross to the right (over 4 vertical threads and the upright stitch) into mesh 3. Bring needle up in mesh 4 to position for the next unit. Cross stitches (page 44) are worked in the spaces between the cross-and-bar units, often in a finer yarn and/or different color.

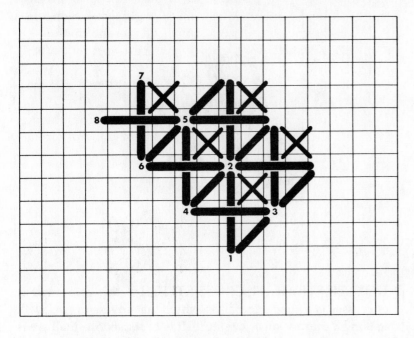

Stitch Guide		
	from	to
first	1	2
unit	1	3
	4	3
second	4	5
unit	4	2
	6	2

DOUBLE STITCH — a combination stitch that's pretty in two colors or two different textures. It gives good coverage of the canvas when yarn is adjusted to proper fullness (a thinner yarn may be used for the small crosses). This is a utility stitch, good for filling. Works fairly fast.

First, work Oblong Cross stitches (page 52) over 1 vertical and 3 horizontal threads. Work from right to left in horizontal encroaching rows. Then work single Cross stitches (page 44) *between* the oblong crosses. Be sure all top stitches of all crosses are slanted in the same direction.

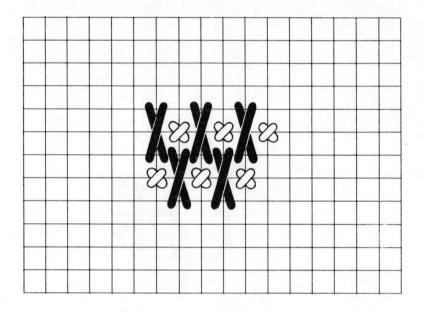

DOUBLE STRAIGHT CROSS STITCH — this combination of crosses is a good general-use stitch that covers canvas well, making a bumpy surface texture. It is best used in small areas because it's a great wool-user. Works fast.

Each unit consists of an upright cross over 4 threads (shown as the dark crosses on the diagram), topped with a slanted cross over 2 threads (the lighter crosses on the diagram). Work in horizontal rows from left to right, completing each unit before going on to the next. The second row fits into the first. Take care — the top stitches of each unit should slant in the same direction.

If using two colors, work all the upright crosses first. Then, working from right to left, make the smaller crosses in your second color. (See Cross stitch, page 44.) This method works slowly because each row is worked twice.

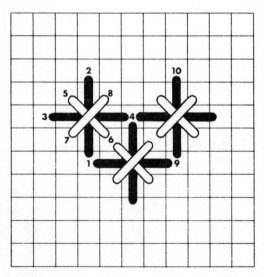

LARGE AND STRAIGHT CROSS STITCH — another combination of crosses that gives a nice decorative surface for general use. Fit the yarn to your canvas — often a thicker yarn may be desired for the large stitches. Works slowly.

First, work entire area with Cross stitches (page 44) over 4 horizontal and vertical threads. Then work Upright Cross stitches (page 61) over 2 horizontal and vertical threads between the large crosses. The upright crosses may be worked in another color and/or a finer yarn. Top stitches should all cross in the same direction.

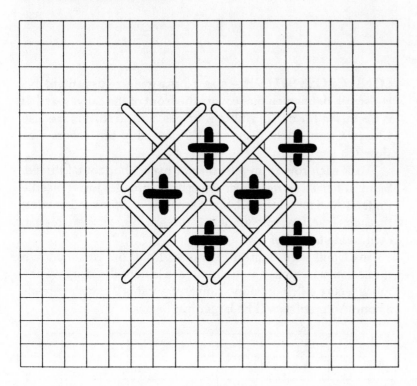

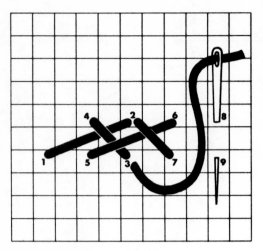

LONG-ARMED CROSS STITCH (Plaited Slav stitch) — a
small utility stitch that covers canvas well, making a thick, ribbed face and small, even stitches on the back. Works fast.

Work each row from left to right over 2 horizontal threads. Slant stitch *up to right* over 4 vertical threads (needle at back is vertical under 2 threads), slant stitch *up to left* over 2 vertical threads (needle at back is vertical under 2 threads); repeat these two stitches to end of row. Start next row at the left, 2 threads below last row. Remember, the long arm *always* slants up from left to right; needle at back is *always* vertical.

Stitch Guide

from	to
1	2
3	4
5	6
7	2
3	8
9	

LONG CROSS STITCH — classed as a general-use stitch, this
is a small, tight stitch that covers the front of the canvas well. It is best used for detail, ribbing, stripes, and so forth. (See also Closed Cross stitch, page 44.) Works easily but covers area slowly.

Work each row from left to right over 1 horizontal thread. Slant stitch *up to right* over 2 vertical threads, insert needle under 1 horizontal thread, slant stitch *up to left* over 2 vertical threads, insert needle under 1 thread intersection; repeat, continuing to end of row.

Don't pull yarn tight or canvas will pull out of shape. On mono canvas, stitches may slip if yarn is not full enough. For a more secure stitch on mono canvas, try using 2 canvas threads as one. Your stitch will be larger but firmer.

Stitch Guide

from	to
1	2
3	4
5	6
7	8
3	9
10	2
7	11
12	6
10	13

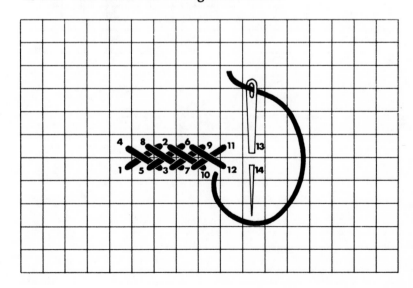

LONG-LEGGED CROSS STITCH

LONG-LEGGED CROSS STITCH — like the Long-Armed Cross stitch (page 50), this is a small utility stitch that makes a firm, hard-wearing ribbed surface. Works fast.

Work each row from left to right over 2 horizontal threads. Slant stitch *up to right* over 2 vertical threads (needle at back is horizontal under 2 vertical threads), slant stitch *down to right* over 4 vertical threads; repeat to end of row. Long arm *always* slants down from left to right; at the back, needle is *always* horizontal under 2 vertical threads — first at top, then at bottom of row.

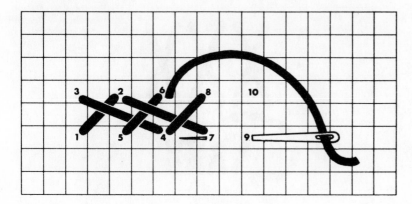

<table>
<thead>
<tr><th colspan="2">Stitch Guide</th></tr>
<tr><th>from</th><th>to</th></tr>
</thead>
<tbody>
<tr><td>1</td><td>2</td></tr>
<tr><td>3</td><td>4</td></tr>
<tr><td>5</td><td>6</td></tr>
<tr><td>2</td><td>7</td></tr>
<tr><td>4</td><td>8</td></tr>
<tr><td>6</td><td>9</td></tr>
<tr><td>7</td><td></td></tr>
</tbody>
</table>

MONTENEGRIN CROSS STITCH

MONTENEGRIN CROSS STITCH — an old stitch, not too often used today, that makes a pretty background surface. It covers canvas well and is good for general use. It gives a tweedy, ribbed texture on the front and makes an even, regular stitch on the back. Works easily once you get the rhythm of the stitches.

Similar to Long-Armed Cross stitch (page 50) and Long-Legged Cross stitch (above), this too is worked from the left in rows over 2 horizontal threads.

Begin by slanting a long stitch *up to right* over 4 vertical threads. Bring needle up 2 meshes to right of mesh 1 and slant stitch *up to left* over 2 vertical threads. Bring needle up in the same mesh again (3) and make upright stitch over 2 horizontal threads. Bring needle up again in mesh 3 and slant a long stitch *up to right* over 4 vertical threads. These last three stitches complete the irregular unit — short arm, upright bar, and long arm — all worked from the same mesh. Bring needle up in mesh 7 to begin next irregular unit. Continue to end of row. Begin next row at the left, 2 threads below the row just completed.

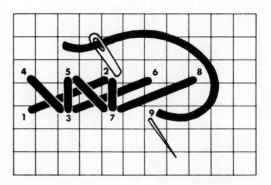

<table>
<thead>
<tr><th colspan="2">Stitch Guide</th></tr>
<tr><th>from</th><th>to</th></tr>
</thead>
<tbody>
<tr><td>1</td><td>2</td></tr>
<tr><td>3</td><td>4</td></tr>
<tr><td>3</td><td>5</td></tr>
<tr><td>3</td><td>6</td></tr>
<tr><td>7</td><td>5</td></tr>
<tr><td>7</td><td>2</td></tr>
<tr><td>7</td><td>8</td></tr>
<tr><td>9</td><td></td></tr>
</tbody>
</table>

OBLONG CROSS STITCH — a Cross stitch for general use. This is a fairly open stitch, so some canvas may show. Adjust wool to preferred fullness for your canvas. Works fast.

This stitch can be worked over almost any thread count, but it is usually done over 4 horizontal and 2 vertical threads. Work in horizontal rows from right to left. Be sure to cross all stitches in the same direction.

Stitch Guide

from	to
1	2
3	4
3	5
6	2
6	

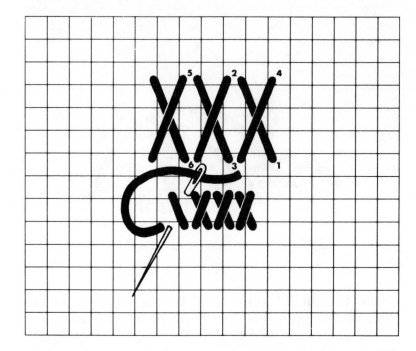

OBLONG CROSS WITH BACK STITCH — similar to the Oblong Cross stitch (above), but with an added Back stitch (page 34) in the same or a contrasting color to tie down the center of each cross. (A Back stitch may also be worked at the base of each cross.) This stitch can be worked over and back without turning the canvas. Easy to work, but it takes a bit more time because of the tie stitch.

When working in one color, three stitches complete each unit (see diagram).

If working two colors, first work rows of Oblong Cross stitches from right to left. Then, with second color, make the Back stitches, working from right to left.

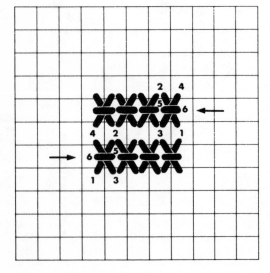

REVERSED CROSS STITCH — a large and decorative pattern stitch of alternating slanted and upright crosses. This stitch is a little slow to work, but it covers an area quickly. (It works faster on a frame.)

First, for the underlying layer of stitches, alternate large slanted and upright crosses over 4 vertical and horizontal threads in the entire area to be covered (shown as dark stitches on the diagram).

Then, when area is covered, stitch over each cross with another cross in the opposite direction (shown as the lighter crosses on the diagram).

Try a fairly thick yarn for the first crosses. The second or top crosses may be worked in a contrasting color and/or kind of yarn — for instance, try silk, cotton, or bouclé.

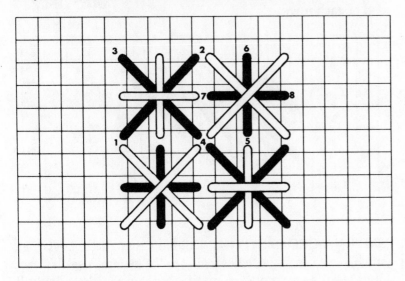

ST. GEORGE AND ST. ANDREW CROSS STITCH — another pattern stitch of alternating slanted and upright crosses. It makes an interesting surface texture for general use, and is also good in two shades of wool. But one caution — yarn must be full enough or canvas will peek through. Works fairly slowly.

Each cross is worked over 2 vertical and horizontal threads. Works easily in diagonal rows from top left to bottom right. Complete diagonal rows of cross stitches first, then work upright crosses in diagonal rows to fill in the spaces between the regular cross stitches.

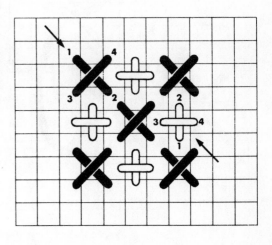

SLANTING CROSS STITCH — a novelty stitch usually chosen for its decorative quality or for special effects. It is excellent in two colors. Works up fairly quickly.

Work in horizontal rows, starting at the left. The first short stitch on the diagram is a fill-in stitch to square off the corner. Pattern stitch begins in mesh 1 and slants *up to right* over 4 horizontal and vertical threads. In base row, skip 1 mesh and then slant next stitch up to right; continue across row, skipping 1 mesh between each stitch. Don't pull stitches tight.

On return row (don't turn canvas), make upright stitches. Work each upright stitch from the open (skipped) mesh between each slanted stitch, first from the top down and then from the bottom up (as indicated by arrows on diagram). To finish the area, make short fill-in stitches at the beginning or end of each row.

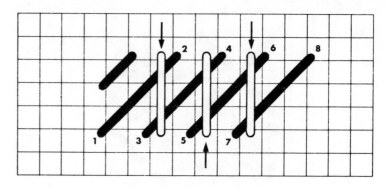

SMYRNA CROSS STITCH (Double Cross stitch, Leviathan stitch) — an old favorite belonging to the general-use class but often used as a decorative motif. Works up fairly quickly if working in one color.

Work in horizontal rows, working each unit over 4 vertical and horizontal threads. Make a regular cross first, then top with an upright cross. Be sure all upright crosses are crossed in the same direction. If working in one color, complete each unit before going on to the next (see diagram). If working in two colors, work regular crosses across row from right to left; then work return row in upright crosses in second color.

This stitch can also be worked over just 2 threads, or over as many as 6 to 8 threads. However, the larger the stitch, the more open the pattern — so the more the canvas will show. (Sometimes fill-in stitches are added.) Larger units are often prettier if worked with a fuller yarn (more plies).

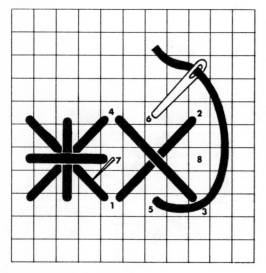

SQUARED-OFF CROSS STITCH (Check stitch) — a large novelty stitch usually used as a single motif, although it can be used as a decorative background stitch. As a repeat in an area, it must be worked to fit the area exactly; this is one of the stitches which must be counted carefully, so count (and mark) the threads to be sure. This stitch works up full and puffy on the front, with little coverage on the back. Works slowly.

Each arm of the cross consists of three stitches worked over 6 and 2 threads. As with all cross stitches, be sure all units are crossed in the same direction.

On mono canvas, stitches may slip if the yarn is not full enough or it is pulled too tight. It is advisable on mono canvas to position the first unit (by counting the threads) so that when the needle is put into the canvas at position "4-5" it goes *under* a "held-down" thread (see page 22).

TIED-DOWN CROSS STITCH — a decorative stitch that must fit exactly into the selected area; count (and mark) the canvas threads for exact fit. This stitch may also be used as a motif stitch or worked *on top* of an area of basic Tent stitches to give accent or texture. It makes a closely covered front surface, with little coverage on the back. Works up slowly, but is so effective it is worth the time.

Work in diagonal rows from top left to bottom right. The long arms (three stitches to each unit) may be worked over 4 or 6 threads. Don't pull long arms tight or it will draw canvas out of shape.

To prevent slipping on mono canvas, position the first stitch so that when needle is put into the canvas at position "2-3" it goes *under* a "held-down" thread (see page 22).

To tie down the long arms, work a small Upright Cross stitch (page 61) over 2 vertical and horizontal threads. If using a contrasting color for the tying cross, it is easier if a second needle threaded in the contrasting color is used. Complete each unit before starting the next.

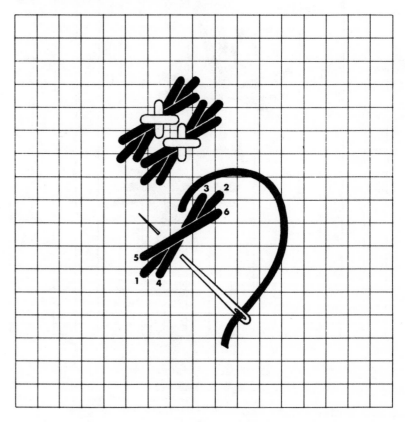

TRAMMED CROSS STITCH — in Tramé work (see Tramé stitch, page 144), long stitches are laid along the filling (horizontal) threads of the canvas and then worked over with any of several stitches — here, with Cross stitches (page 44). This stitch may be worked in two colors. Works easily but slowly.

Lay Tramé first. The length of the Tramé stitches should vary so that joining won't show on the front of the canvas. Work from left to right, inserting needle under 1 vertical thread between each long Tramé stitch. Or, for extra holding, split Tramé stitch as yarn is needled under vertical threads (see Split Tramé stitch, page 143). When working on penelope canvas, lay Tramé between 1 double thread.

Then work Cross stitches over canvas threads and the Tramé, working from right to left.

For a different look, try working this stitch vertically, or use a thick yarn for the Tramé and a regular yarn for the crosses. If Tramé is very full, skip 1 or 2 meshes between each Cross stitch.

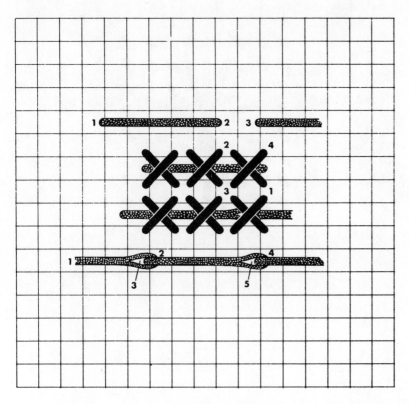

TRIPLE CROSS STITCH — a large motif stitch that is most effective when it is planned to fit exactly into an area. It works best and looks smoothest if the area is filled in first with the basic Tent stitch, leaving unworked the exact number of threads needed for the motif. Work this stitch with great care for best results. Works slowly.

Two groups of three stitches make up each of the large crosses. Work the first group vertically (1-6 on the diagram), and the second group horizontally (7-12 on the diagram). The long center stitch of each covers 8 threads; the two slanted stitches each cross the center stitch and cover 6 threads.

With the same or a contrasting color, make the small center cross over 2 vertical and horizontal threads (13-16 on the diagram). The top (last) stitch should slant from bottom left to upper right.

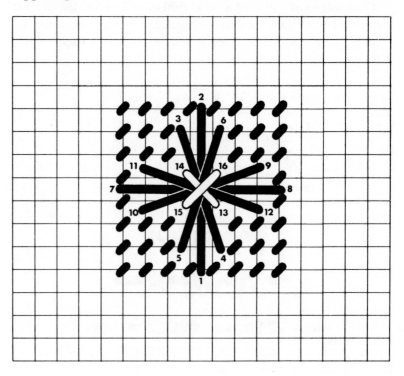

TWO-SIDED CROSS STITCH (Reversible Cross stitch) — an embroidery stitch that can be used on canvas for special effects. This is a fairly open decorative stitch, looking the same on both the front and back of the canvas. The canvas may show through, so adjust thickness of yarn for desired coverage. Worked in horizontal rows starting at the left, it requires four journeys to complete one row. Works slowly.

Beginning at the left, slant stitch *up to right* over 4 vertical and horizontal threads on the front of the canvas, then slant stitch at back *down to right* under 4 vertical and horizontal threads; repeat across row. Make a small half-stitch on bottom leg of last cross to position needle for return journey. Work back in the same manner, crossing stitches made on the first journey. For the third journey, work as for first, but this time fill in the spaces between the crosses already worked; make a half-stitch to turn, to position needle for fourth journey (follow Stitch Guide and diagram). Concentration is needed to work this one!

Stitch Guide

	from	to
first journey	1	2
	3	4
	5	6
	7	8 — ½ stitch
second journey	7	9 — ½ stitch
	10	11
	12	13
third journey	12	11
	10	9
	8	7 — ½ stitch
fourth journey	5	4
	3	2
	1	14 — ½ stitch

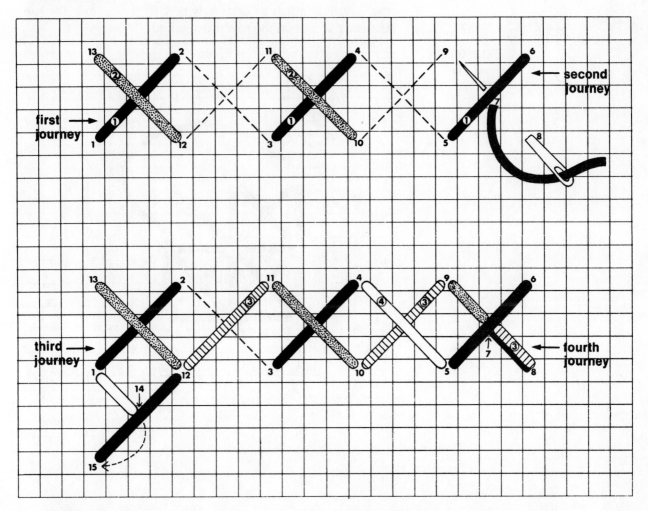

TWO-SIDED ITALIAN CROSS STITCH (Arrowhead stitch) — a small general-use stitch that can be decorative in large areas. It covers canvas well if yarn is full. This stitch can be very effective, and it's fun to do because it works easily and fast after a little practice.

Work in horizontal rows from left to right, *bottom to top.*

First stitch: Bring needle up (mesh 1) and make a straight stitch to the right over 3 vertical threads (mesh 2). **Second stitch:** Bring needle up again in mesh 1 and slant stitch *up to right* over 3 vertical and horizontal threads to mesh 3. **Third stitch:** Again from mesh 1, make an upright stitch over 3 horizontal threads to mesh 4. **Fourth stitch:** From mesh 2, slant stitch *up to left,* crossing the second stitch, into mesh 4. Bring needle up again in mesh 2. Repeat units to end of row. If row ends in a whole unit, a finishing upright stitch should be added. If row ends in a partial stitch, a half unit can be worked, or fill-in Tent stitches can be used.

Start the next row at the left again, just *above* the completed row. The first stitch of each new row then becomes the top stitch of the unit on the row just worked.

Stitch Guide

from	to
1	2
1	3
1	4
2	4
2	

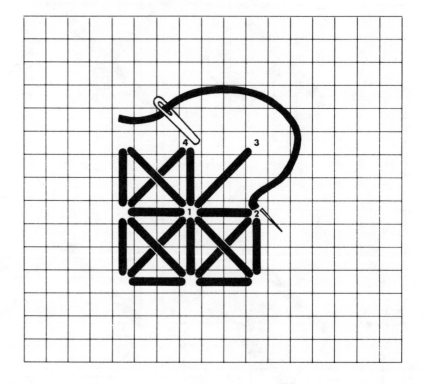

UPRIGHT CROSS STITCH (Straight Cross stitch) — a good small utility stitch that covers canvas well and gives an even, hard-wearing, nubby surface. Adjust yarn to fit canvas — for example, try 2-ply Persian wool on 10 count canvas. Works fast.

Work in interlocking horizontal rows over 2 vertical and horizontal threads. Always cross the upright stitch so that the horizontal stitch is on top.

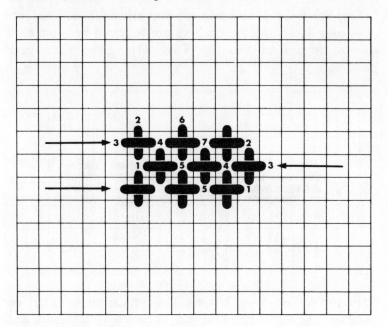

Stitch Guide

	from	to
over	1	2
	3	4
	5	6
	4	7
back	1	2
	3	4
	5	7
	4	5

(end of Cross Stitches)

DAMASK STITCH

A slanting flat stitch that could be included under either the Gobelin or Satin stitches, this stitch is a wool-user. It's excellent for large areas, background, or filling, and it is very nice for shading. Works fairly fast.

Like the Encroaching Gobelin stitch (page 88), work horizontal rows from the top of the canvas, working each row across from left to right. Slant stitch up to right over 4 horizontal and 2 vertical threads. The next row starts at the left again, 2 threads under the last row, and encroaches the last row by 2 threads. Other counts, such as 6 or 8 threads, can be worked out for special effects.

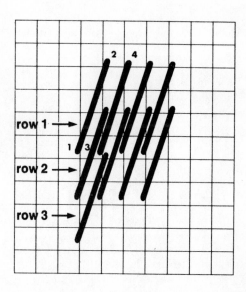

DARNING STITCH

This stitch is an old utility stitch often used for filling in certain types of embroidery. It can be adapted for special effects in backgrounds and smaller areas on canvas work. It can be used in rugs, too, if it is worked tightly enough with full yarn. Usually a heavy wool-user, this stitch works slowly.

From 3 to 6 threads may be "darned" (yarn laid along, then caught under, vertical or horizontal threads) to form patterns. Follow Stitch Guide and diagram for basic method; two journeys over and two journeys back are required between each pair of horizontal threads. (This form gives good back padding.)

Stitch Guide

	from	to
over	1	2
	3	4
back	5	4
	3	2
over	1	2
	3	4
back	5	4
	3	2

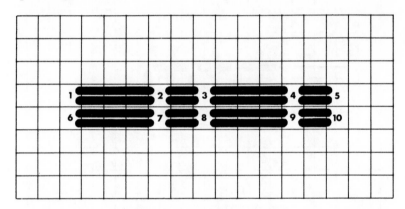

Variation A: Two-Way Darning. The vertical stitches (dark on diagram) are worked into the canvas over 6 to 12 threads and under 1 thread. The horizontal stitches (light on diagram) are darned in a regular count over 2 darned and 3 canvas threads and under 2 darned threads and 1 canvas thread. The horizontal darning may be in a different color.

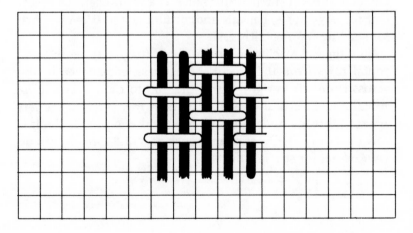

Variation B: Darning plus Tent stitch. The rows of Darning stitches are irregularly spaced but are *all* over 3 threads and under 1 thread in this example (other counts may be used). The placement is irregular to give an irregular or tweedy effect. The Tent stitches are worked after the darning is completed, and may be in a different color.

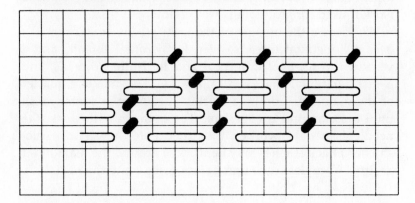

Variation C: Two-Way Darning. This may be worked in two colors or one. Since it is easiest to work darning from right to left, begin at the top right. Work horizontal rows over 4 and under 2 threads across row. Make three rows. On the next three rows, alternate placement of the groups of stitches (light stitches on diagram). Continue alternating horizontal groups of three rows until the area is covered. To work the vertical stitches (dark on diagram), give the canvas a quarter turn and with the same or a second color work groups of three horizontal rows with stitches covering the open spaces of the darned area.

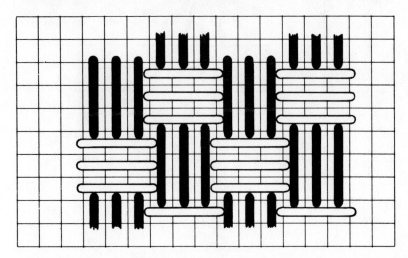

DIAGONAL TENT STITCH (see Basic Tent Stitch, page 28)

DIAMOND EYELET STITCH

This motif stitch can be used alone or in groups. Adjust yarn thickness for best coverage of canvas — try a 2-ply strand of 3-ply Persian wool on 10 count canvas. This stitch is tedious to work if used for grounding. Works slowly.

Work from the outside of the unit *into* the center mesh — over 4 horizontal threads, over 3 horizontal threads and 1 vertical thread, over 2 vertical and horizontal threads, and over 1 horizontal and 3 vertical threads. This makes a quarter of the diamond. Continue working around the center mesh until the diamond is complete. (For even, smooth work, the needle is always worked into the center mesh in eyelet stitches.) Back stitches may be worked around the diamond if desired. Complete each unit before going on to the next.

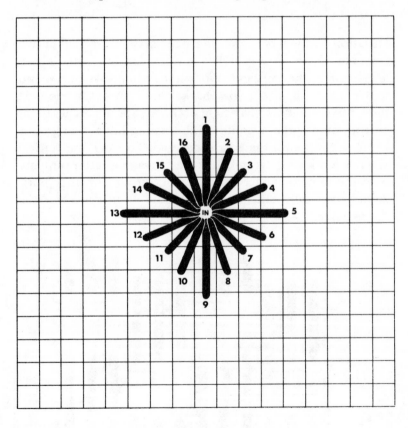

DOUBLE BASKET WEAVE STITCH

This is a novelty stitch that uses the diagonal working method. It makes an irregular, tweedy surface texture, pretty for filling or background, and with a combination of colors, a decorative stripe. Don't pull stitches tight — this stitch pulls canvas quite crooked while being worked. Works fairly fast.

Use a slanted stitch over 2 thread intersections in the same manner as the Diagonal Tent or Basket Weave stitch (page 29), but note that there are two *extra* Tent stitches at the end of each row to keep edges even and bring needle easily to position for the following row. Work in diagonal rows, from the top down (dark stitches on diagram) and from the bottom up (light stitches on diagram). Follow the Stitch Guide until you get the rhythm.

Note: This stitch will be much easier to work if the basic Basket Weave stitch has already been mastered.

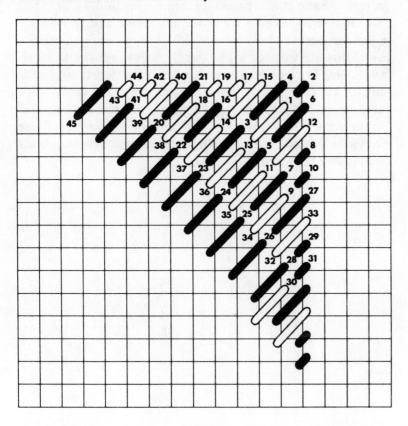

Stitch Guide		
	from	to
down	1	2
	3	4
	5	6
	7	8
	9	10
up	11	12
	13	1
	14	15
	16	17
	18	19
down	20	21
	22	16
	23	3
	24	5
	25	

DOUBLE SATIN STAR STITCH

Here, a large decorative stitch is worked in two parts. The outer unit is Satin stitch; the center, a novelty cross stitch. This stitch can be used alone, or to make a handsome central motif for a geometric or modern design. Works slowly.

The Double Star must be planned to fit the area exactly; use a needlepoint marker or sewing thread to mark off a square area of, say, 17 horizontal and vertical threads. The size of the Double Star may be varied — just take care to count off the area required and mark it to make stitching easier.

Work the center first (light stitches on diagram) — over 3 horizontal and vertical threads. Make two upright stitches, then cross them with two horizontal stitches. Work a Cross stitch over the straight stitches, starting in the mesh below the last horizontal stitch.

The outer star (dark stitches on diagram) is worked in four groups of Satin stitch (page 129). Starting with the unit at top of center, bring needle up 2 meshes above and to right of upper left corner of center unit. Work three upright stitches over 5 threads, the second and third stitches each from 1 mesh below and to right of previous stitch. The fourth and fifth stitches are each over 4 threads. Then finish the group with three upright stitches over 5 threads, with the seventh and eighth each 1 mesh up from the previous stitch. Continue clockwise around center, making three more Satin stitch units to complete the motif.

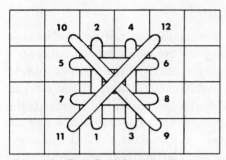

Detail of Center

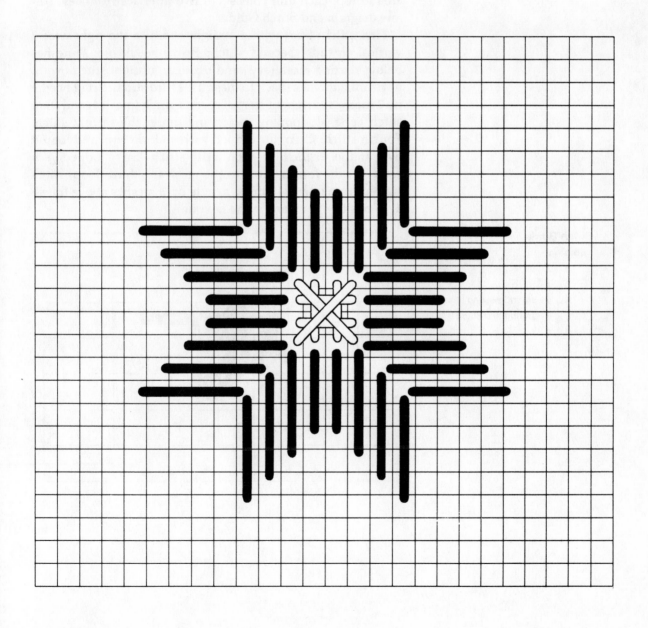

EASTERN STITCH

Eastern stitch is an intricate stitch that isn't often used but can be most effective as a filling texture or an overlaid accent. It makes a hard, close, bumpy surface when worked over 2 threads, and covers canvas well on both sides. When worked over 4 (or more) threads, the surface is softly textured; the stitch is usually used this way as a decorative overlay on finished needlepoint. This is a big wool-user. Works slowly.

Work in horizontal rows from left to right, from bottom of area to top. Each unit consists of five interlaced stitches. Follow diagram and Stitch Guide.

First stitch: Start with a straight stitch to the right over 2 vertical threads. **Second stitch:** Bring needle up 2 meshes below starting mesh (at 3) and make an upright stitch over 2 horizontal threads (back to mesh 1). **Third stitch:** Bring needle up 2 meshes to right of start of second stitch (mesh 4) and slant stitch *up to left*, looping it *over* and under the second stitch. **Fourth stitch:** Carry the looped yarn *up to the right* and loop it over and *under* the first stitch. **Fifth stitch:** Carry looped yarn *down over* the fourth stitch to the mesh the third (loop) stitch started from (mesh 4). Bring needle up 2 meshes above (mesh 2) to position for starting the next unit.

Stitch Guide

from	to	
1	2	
3	1	
4	5	around second stitch
5	6	around first stitch
6	4	
2		

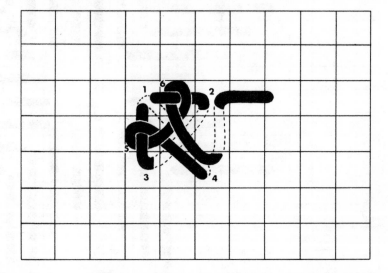

ENCROACHING OBLIQUE STITCH

This is a close, slanting stitch for general use. It can be worked in-the-hand, but for best results should be worked on a frame. (If working in-the-hand, take care not to pull stitches tight — the canvas tends to pull very crooked with this stitch.) Covers canvas well, making a pretty, smooth surface. Works fast.

Work in horizontal rows over and back, top to bottom. Starting at the left, slant stitch *down to right* over 1 horizontal and 4 vertical threads. Bring needle up 2 meshes to right of first stitch and continue to end of area.

The return row reverses this procedure — slant stitch *up to left* over 1 horizontal and 4 vertical threads, bringing needle up 2 meshes to left of last stitch.

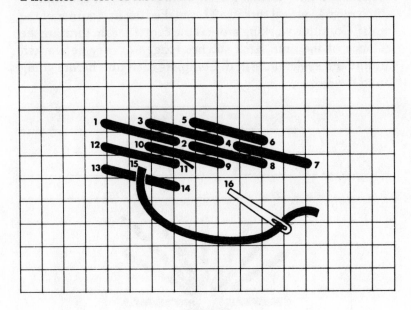

Stitch Guide

	from	to
over	1	2
	3	4
	5	6
back	7	4
	8	2
	9	10
	11	12

EYE STITCH

This medium-large motif stitch may be used alone or as a repeat in an area. (See also Diamond Eyelet stitch, page 64.) Adjust yarn thickness to fit your canvas. Works slowly.

Mark off a square area of 8 horizontal and vertical threads. Work each stitch from the outside of the unit *into* the center mesh. (For even, smooth work, the needle is always worked into the center mesh in eyelet stitches.) The first stitch is a straight stitch from the top to the center over 4 horizontal threads. The second stitch is slanted over 2 vertical and 4 horizontal threads. The third stitch is slanted over 4 vertical and horizontal threads. The fourth stitch is slanted over 4 vertical and 2 horizontal threads. The fifth stitch is a straight stitch over 4 vertical threads. This makes the first corner of the motif. Continue working around the center mesh, forming the balance of the unit. Back stitches (page 34) may be worked around the eyelet if desired. Complete each unit before going on to the next.

Variation: Irregular eyelets may be used to advantage in groundings or as accent motifs. Two or more colors may be worked into one eyelet or eyelet group.

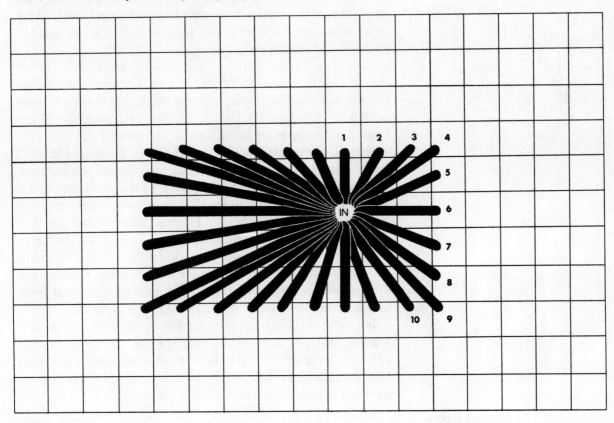

FEATHER STITCH (Coral stitch)

An embroidery stitch that is worked over Tramé when adapted for canvas work (see Tramé stitch, page 144), this stitch covers the surface well with bumpy ridges. It is best for small areas, special effects, and small stripes; it's also good in two colors. Works slowly.

First, lay Tramé between every *other* horizontal canvas thread. Work the Feather stitch over 2 horizontal canvas threads and the laid stitch, taking a stitch first from top, then bottom of row. For the first stitch (for best coverage of the beginning of the row), bring needle up in mesh above Tramé (mesh 3), bring yarn down to right over Tramé, hold with thumb, and take a small stitch *up* under 1 thread intersection, bringing needle out *over* the yarn held by thumb (see diagram **a**). Bring yarn to right, hold with thumb, carry yarn up to left and take a stitch down under 1 thread intersection (see diagram **b**) with needle coming out over yarn held by thumb to form second stitch. Bring yarn down to right, hold with thumb, take a small stitch up under 1 intersection. Continue to end of area by repeating these two open stitches, first from above, then from below the laid yarn (see diagram **c**).

If you're working in-the-hand rather than on a frame, it may be easier to work if you turn the canvas so the Feather stitch is worked from top to bottom after the Tramé has been laid. (But if you do this, be sure to turn canvas back to original position to continue working other stitches!)

Stitch Guide

from	to
1	2
3	4
5	6
7	8
7	9
10	11
10	12
13	14
13	15

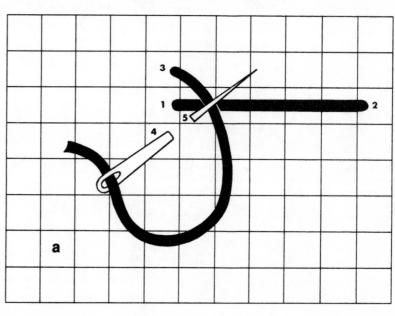

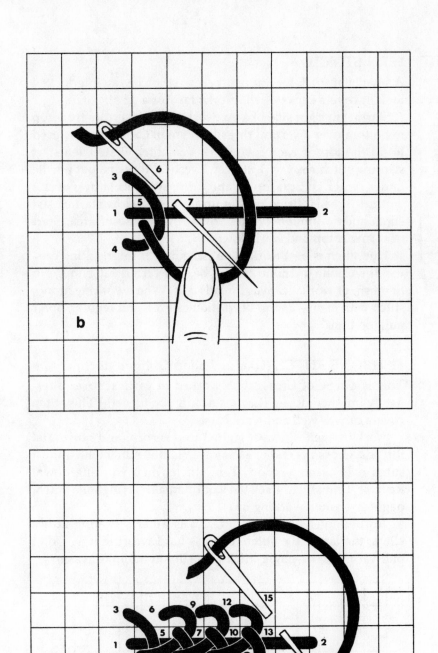

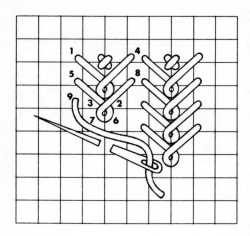

FERN STITCH

A small, flat stitch for utility use, Fern stitch has an interlocked look. It covers canvas well. Works fast for a small stitch.

Starting at right side of area, work in vertical rows from top to bottom over 3 vertical threads. A small Cross stitch is used to fill the top of each row; work this stitch first. Then start slanting stitch *down to right* over 2 vertical threads, put needle under center vertical thread and bring stitch *up to right* over 2 vertical threads. Bring needle up in mesh below start of last stitch and continue working down row to end of area. Start next row at top and work down.

This stitch is best worked on penelope or interlocking canvas. If working on mono canvas, be sure yarn is full enough to fit mesh, or work 2 canvas threads as 1. When working mono, stitch with care — and to keep stitches even and regular, don't pull too tight.

FISHBONE STITCH (Long and Short Oblique stitch)

This is a type of Cross stitch worked in vertical rows: alternately up, then down. (Canvas needn't be turned.) This stitch covers canvas well and works fast.

Work in even ribs over from 3 to 6 vertical and horizontal threads. Cross the end of each long, slanted stitch with a short stitch over 1 intersection (Tent stitch when working down, Reverse Tent stitch — see the Continental Herringbone stitch, page 92 — when working up).

Worked over a small count, this is a hard-wearing utility stitch; the larger the stitch, the less hard wearing it is. Don't pull yarn tight or single stitch may slip on mono canvas.

Stitch Guide

	from	to
up	1	2
	3	4
	5	6
	7	2
	8	9
	10	6
down	11	8
	12	13
	14	5
	15	8
	16	1
	17	5

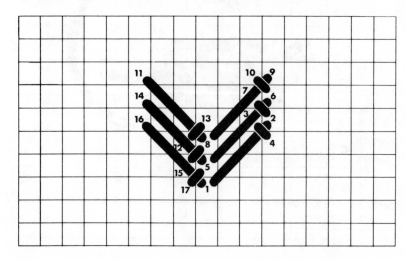

FLORENCE STITCH (German stitch)

A good general-use and utility stitch, this is a flat stitch that covers canvas well, and is good for combining colors. It is sometimes used as a variation of the Diagonal Mosaic stitch (page 108). Works fast.

Work in diagonal rows from bottom right to top left. Stitches slant up to the right, alternating over 1, then 2 intersections. The second row fits into the first (see diagram **a**).

This stitch can also be worked over 2, then 3 intersections (see diagram **b**).

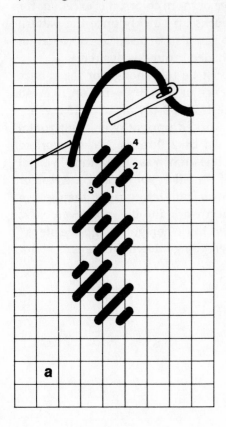

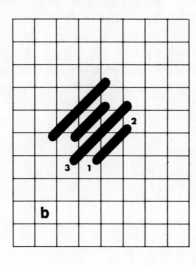

Florentine Embroidery

Florentine embroidery, a special type of canvas work that was very popular in Florence, Italy, was originally used for upholstery, draperies, and accessories. Today, the Florentine stitch is used alone or in combination with other needlepoint stitches for interesting effects. All stitches are upright, and when color contrasts and shadings are used, beautiful patterns can be made.

BARGELLO STITCH — a type of Florentine embroidery. Prettiest when worked in five or more colors, it is excellent for shading, wears well, and works up quickly once the pattern line is established. Bargello can also be used in combination with needlepoint where a shaded ground is desired.

For Bargello, the wool must be full enough or the canvas will peek through. If using Persian yarn, try 4-ply on 10 mesh canvas, 3-ply on 12 or 14 mesh, and 2-ply on 16 or 18 mesh.

All Bargello stitches are worked upright over 4 horizontal threads and raised or lowered by 2 threads. (When worked over fewer or more threads, it is known as "Florentine" work.) The stitches form rows of steplike points and curves, or geometric patterns. Work rows from left to right, then return right to left. For the smoothest work and the most even back, work stitches from bottom to top when going "up the steps" and from top to bottom when going "down the steps."

Stitch Guide

	from	to
up	1	2
	3	4
down	5	6
	7	8
	9	10
up	11	12
	13	14

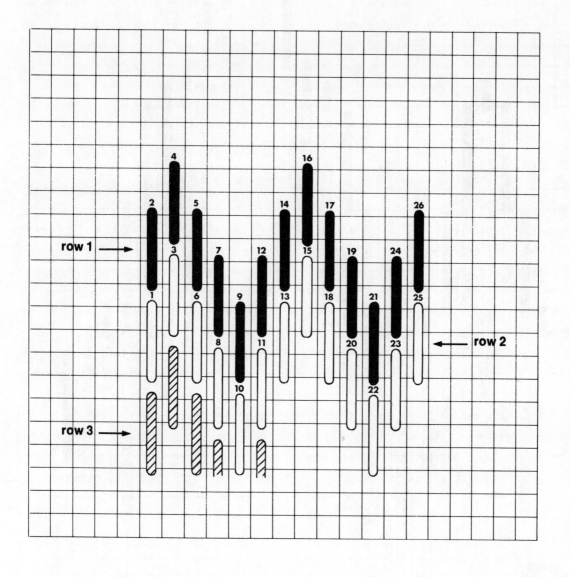

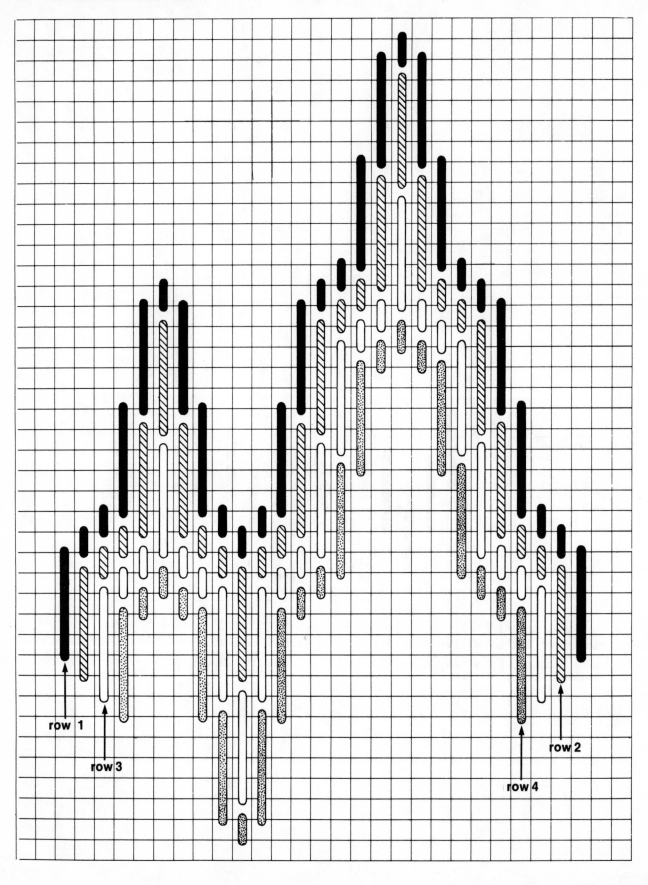

row 1

row 3

row 2

row 4

FLORENTINE STITCH (Flame stitch) — this stitch can really be classed as a separate type of canvas work. Florentine patterns are usually large, so are prettiest when worked with from five to ten or more colors. Yarn must be full enough to cover the canvas completely. Florentine stitch is often used for chair or sofa upholstery as well as for smaller items like footstools and travel bags. Works up fairly quickly once the pattern line is established.

Many Florentine patterns are traditional; they date back several hundred years and have specific names. It is possible to count (copy) a pattern from an old piece of needlework or from a chart; after some practice, you can work out your own designs. No two patterns are alike and there is an almost endless variety — Florentine work is a fascinating world of its own.

The upright stitch for Florentine work is most often worked over 2, 4, or 6 horizontal threads. Although it may be worked over more threads, remember that the longer the stitch, the less wear the embroidery will give, for it will snag more easily. Also, in Florentine work, a stitch or group of stitches may be raised (or lowered) by any number of threads — 1, 2, 3, 4, or 5. This makes the sharp points or deep curves of a pattern.

Sometimes Florentine stitch counts or ratios are given in instructions as 4-1, 6-2, 6-3, and so on. The first number is the number of threads the stitch is worked over; the second number indicates the number of threads the needle comes back *under* to be in position to make the next stitch.

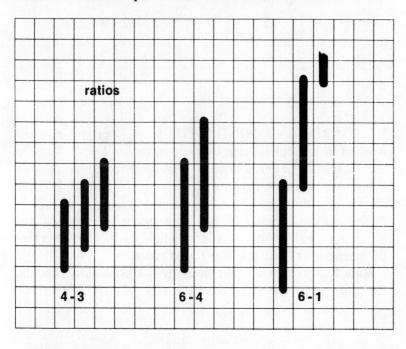

ratios

4 - 3   6 - 4   6 - 1

HUNGARIAN STITCH — a small, upright stitch in the Florentine group. It makes a smooth surface and is a good general-use stitch for large areas, such as background and filling. Yarn must be full for this stitch or canvas will show through (add another ply if necessary). Works fast.

Work in horizontal rows over and back; there's no need to turn the canvas. Working from left to right, make a short upright stitch over 2 horizontal threads. Make second, longer upright stitch 1 mesh below and to right of first stitch, over 4 horizontal threads. Make short third stitch upright over 2 horizontal threads, same as first. Skip 1 mesh and repeat this three-stitch unit; continue across row in this manner. The return row fits into the first row, with each short stitch meeting a short stitch and the long stitches worked in the open mesh between the stitch units of the row above.

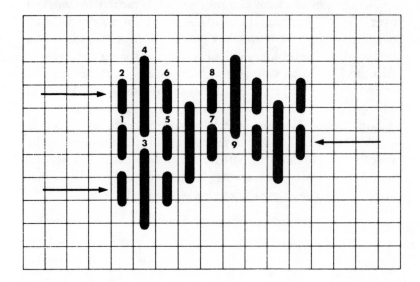

HUNGARIAN GROUND STITCH — upright stitches worked in a motif pattern that combines well with Bargello and Florentine patterns or with Tent stitch for covering large areas prettily and quickly. Be sure wool is full enough to cover canvas.

The pattern consists of two long zigzag rows of stitches enclosing small motifs of four stitches each. Most needlepointers prefer to do the long zigzag rows first.

Row 1: Make an upright stitch over 4 horizontal threads. Bring needle up 1 mesh above and to right of start of first stitch and make the next stitch *up* over 4 threads. Bring needle up 1 mesh above and to right of start of last stitch and make next stitch *up* over 4 threads. Bring needle up 1 mesh *down* and to right and make next stitch *down* over 4 threads. Bring needle up 1 mesh *down* and to right and make next stitch (like the first) *up* over 4 threads. Continue to end of row.

Row 2: Work like first row, except reverse the direction of the steps. Starting in the same mesh as the first stitch of the last row, make a stitch *down* over 4 horizontal threads. Bring needle up 1 mesh *down* and to right of start of first stitch and make next stitch *down* over 4 threads. Bring needle up 1 mesh *down* and to right of start of last stitch and make stitch *down* over 4 threads. Bring needle up 1 mesh *above* and to right and make next stitch *up* over 4 threads. Continue to end of row. Small diamond-shaped areas are left between the "sawtooth" rows.

Row 3: Fill in the small areas with four upright stitches, each worked over 2 horizontal threads. It is pretty if another color or type of yarn is used. Follow Stitch Guide and diagram.

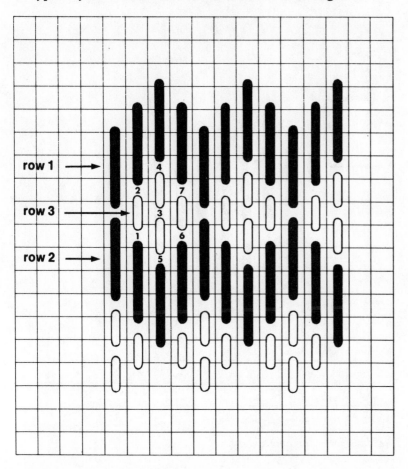

Stitch Guide		
	from	**to**
center	1	2
motif	3	4
	3	5
	6	7

OLD FLORENTINE STITCH (Double Florentine stitch) — a large, loose, upright stitch that is good for background and filling. This stitch needs thick, full yarn to cover canvas completely. Make a sample first — you may want to add 1 or 2 plies of yarn. A nice effect is obtained if the stitch is worked in two colors — for example, the short stitches in one color and the long stitches in another. This is not a hard-wearing stitch, but it covers canvas quickly.

Work horizontal rows from left to right, then return right to left. The stitches are worked in pairs. Start with two stitches, each over 2 horizontal threads, then two stitches, each over 6 threads (2 threads below and 2 above the first pair), then again over 2 threads twice, repeating to end of row. On the return journey the long stitches meet the short stitches, so the rows fit together.

Other counts, such as 3-9-3 or 4-12-4, can also be used, but these larger counts will be more likely to snag — use them for decorative purposes only.

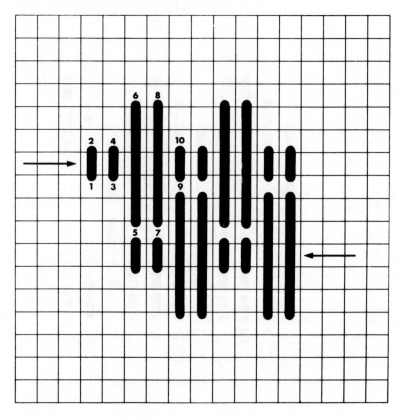

(end of Florentine Embroidery)

FLOWER STITCH

This motif stitch is best used for special effects because it must fit the area exactly. This is a very pretty accent stitch, quite striking in two or three shades. Works slowly.

This stitch must be worked with care. Start in the center, with the Smyrna Cross stitch over 2 vertical and horizontal threads, following the diagram. Next, start working around the center at the upper right corner. Work five stitches, each over 2 threads, working each from the outside *into* mesh 2. Now work the four side stitches that form the long arms. Follow the diagram and Stitch Guide. Continue around the center, working a corner and then a long-arm group until the unit is complete. (For smooth, even work, when several stitches radiate from the same mesh, always work from the outside of the unit *into* that mesh.)

The outside corners that finish this stitch need care too. The *upper right* and *lower left* are Continental stitch (page 28); the *upper left* and *lower right* are Reverse Tent stitch (see Continental Herringbone stitch, page 92).

Stitch Guide

	from	to
long	14	8
arms	15	8
	15	16
	17	8

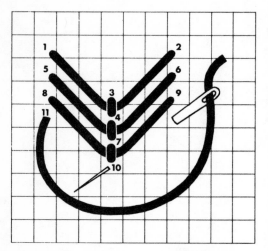

FLY STITCH

A small stitch often found in embroidery, Fly stitch is worked in vertical rows from the top down. This is a nice stitch for filling and background, particularly where a stripe or banding effect is desired. The working method is similar to that for Roman stitch (page 125), but it looks more like Stem stitch (page 142). Works fast.

This stitch may be worked over a count of 4 vertical and 2 horizontal threads, 6 vertical and 3 horizontal threads (as diagrammed), or other counts. From the top, starting at right side of area to be covered, bring needle up to left of the first vertical thread; in one motion, put needle in to right of the sixth vertical thread and bring it up just above the third horizontal thread and between the 2 center vertical threads. To complete each stitch, needle goes in 1 mesh below, over the horizontal thread *and* the yarn, and comes up in mesh below start of stitch (mesh 5), making a small hold stitch over yarn *and* canvas thread. This stitch works easily with two thrusts of the needle when working in-the-hand. Work each new row to left of the preceding row.

FRENCH STITCH

An upright knotted stitch, this looks very small and fine, even when made over 4 threads. Two upright stitches, each tied down in the middle, make each unit. This is a tight stitch, giving a hard-wearing surface. Works fairly quickly after some practice.

Since two stitches are worked into a mesh, yarn should not be too thick — try 2-ply Persian on 10 or 12 count canvas, 1-ply on 14 count. Work diagonal rows from top left to bottom right.

Make upright stitch over 4 horizontal threads. Bring needle up 2 meshes above and 1 mesh to left of start and make tie stitch over vertical canvas thread *and* upright stitch. Bring needle up again in mesh 1, make second upright stitch over 4 horizontal threads, and make tie stitch *from right* (mesh 5) over vertical canvas thread *and* upright stitch into mesh 4. Bring needle up 2 meshes below and 1 to right of mesh 1 to start next unit from mesh 6. Continue in diagonal row to end of area. Next row fits into completed row.

After you're sure of the stitch, for a different effect try working it so the stitches are positioned horizontally.

FRENCH KNOT STITCH

This embroidery stitch is a useful accent stitch. It is often stitched on top of finished needlepoint, although it can be worked right into the canvas. It's good as a single accent — for instance, for an eye or button, or a flower center; it can also be used in clusters to fit a pattern. Works slowly.

Bring yarn up, draw yarn to left and hold taut with thumb and forefinger. Insert point of needle under yarn and twist the held yarn around the needle two or three times, still holding yarn tight; turn needle upward and insert in mesh above and to left (mesh 2 on diagram). Continue to hold yarn taut while pulling needle through to back. The yarn going through the twists forms the knot. This takes a bit of practice, but then the stitch is quite easy to work. The secret is to keep the yarn tight while twisting it around the needle and pulling the stitch through to completion.

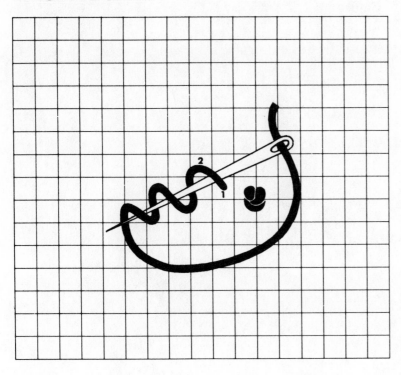

FRINGE STITCH

This stitch belongs to the family of tufted stitches. It is a variation of Surrey Stitch (page 149), and is worked directly on the canvas as a finish for pillows, etc. Wool should be full. Make as many rows (one, two, or three) as necessary to achieve desired fullness. Loops look best if they are 1 inch or more in length; they may be cut to make a fluffier fringe. Loops can be worked in a blend of yarns — for example, wool with strands of silk or bouclé in the same or different colors. Works fast once you get the rhythm.

Work across canvas from left to right. Work rows from the bottom up (on pillow, outside edge) for easiest handling. Skip 1 or 2 meshes between rows, depending on effect desired. On mono canvas, work over 2 threads (as diagrammed); on penelope, over 1 double thread. To start, put needle into the canvas *from the front* at mesh 1. Follow diagrams and Stitch Guide.

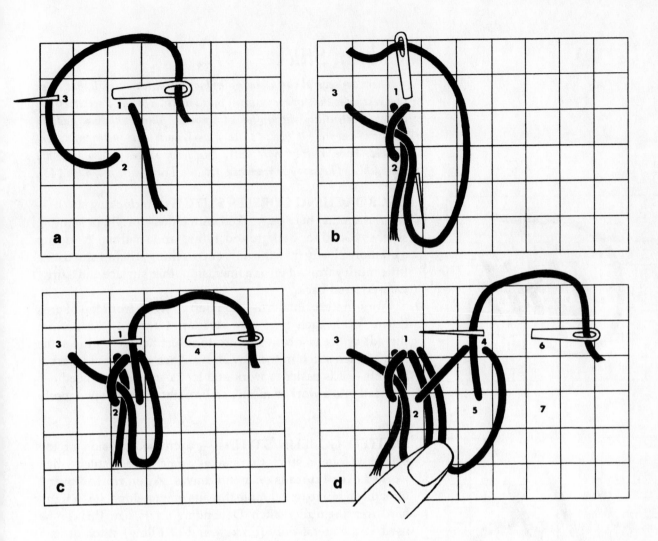

Stitch Guide

from	to	
a. 1	2	Pull tag end down and hold. Carry yarn *up to left*
1	3	to hold at start of row.
b. 1	2	Form loop and hold with thumb. Carry yarn *up to left*
c. 4	1	and pull yarn down tight.
d. 4	5	Form next loop and hold with thumb. Carry yarn *up to left*
6	4	and pull yarn down tight.
6	7	Form loop and continue.

Gobelin Stitches

There are several variations of the Gobelin stitch, a small, flat stitch that resembles the surface weave of the famous Gobelins Tapestries. All are excellent utility stitches for background, filling, shading, and, on occasion, accenting. Gobelin stitches work up a little faster than Tent stitches, have a little more bulk, and form ridges unless they are encroached. They may be trammed, too (see Tramé Stitches, page 143).

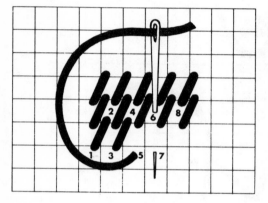

ENCROACHING GOBELIN STITCH (Interlocking stitch) — a variation that may be worked with either upright or slanting stitches. Good for background, filling, and shading. Works up a bit more slowly than the non-encroaching stitches and uses a little more yarn, but gives a finer, smoother surface and a firm, well-covered back.

Work in horizontal rows from left to right, from top of area down. With each new row, overlap 1 thread (the bottom thread) of the last row. Be sure to insert needle on the same side of each stitch in the row above. Each row should start at the left — it is easier to work and looks smoother if needle is inserted into a worked mesh and brought up in an open mesh.

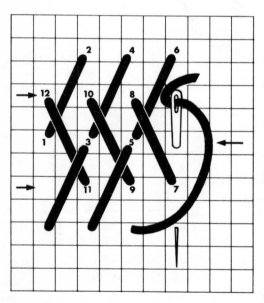

PLAITED GOBELIN STITCH — a crossed version of the Slanting Gobelin stitch that makes a fairly loose stitch when worked over 4 threads on mono canvas. When worked over 2 threads on mono or 2 double threads on penelope, it is a tight, hard-wearing utility stitch. Depending on its size, this can be used as a general-duty (background or filling) stitch or as a decorative stitch. Works quickly and is fun to do.

Work in horizontal rows over and back, reversing the slant of the stitch on the return row. The needle is *always* vertical at the back.

Start at left of area. Slant stitch up to right over 4 horizontal and 2 vertical threads. Bring needle up in second mesh to right of first stitch; slant stitch up to right again. Repeat across row, bringing needle up in every other mesh.

For return row, bring needle up 6 meshes below top of last stitch and slant stitch up to *left* over 4 horizontal and 2 vertical threads, encroaching the first row by 2 threads. Continue across row, slanting each stitch up from second mesh to left of last stitch. The return stitches will cross the stitches in the row above. The alternating slants and encroaching stitches give a plaited look to the surface.

SLANTING GOBELIN STITCH (Gobelin Oblique stitch) — gives a firm, close surface with a fully covered back. This stitch (and the Straight Gobelin stitch) makes a definite ridge on the surface of the canvas. It may be trammed for an even fuller look (see Tramé stitch, page 144). Good for background, filling, and detail. Works fast.

The stitch should be worked from left to right across area to give the most even stitch. Working all rows from left to right uses a bit less yarn and gives the most even back coverage.

Work flat stitches slanting up to right over 2 horizontal threads and 1 vertical thread; bring needle up in next mesh to right for each new stitch. Stitch may also be worked over 3 or 4 horizontal threads.

STRAIGHT GOBELIN STITCH (Gobelin Droit stitch) — an upright stitch used for detail as well as background, filling, and shading. Covers canvas well, but yarn must be full, so add another ply if necessary. Good coverage on the back. Works fast.

Work in horizontal rows over 2, 3, or 4 horizontal threads. The stitch may be worked over and back (no need to turn canvas). If working from the left, bring needle up in next mesh to right of each stitch to make next stitch; reverse procedure if working from the right (return row).

With the longer stitch (over 4 threads), a Back stitch (page 34) in the same or a different color and/or texture yarn is sometimes used between rows.

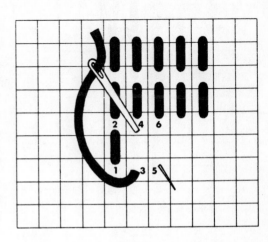

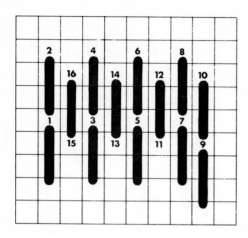

UPRIGHT GOBELIN STITCH — a variation of the Straight Gobelin stitch that is similar to Brick Stitch I (page 37). The stitch is firm and close, and gives a heavy, durable back. Good for background, filling, detail, and shading. Works fast after a bit of practice.

Work in horizontal rows over and back. Working from left to right for first row, make an upright stitch over 3 horizontal threads; skip 1 mesh and make next upright stitch. Continue to end, skipping 1 mesh between each stitch.

For return row, bring needle up 1 mesh below and to right of last stitch — work upright stitches over 3 horizontal threads between stitches of last row. Repeat until area is covered. Return row encroaches previous row by 2 threads; the left to right row encroaches the return row by only 1 thread.

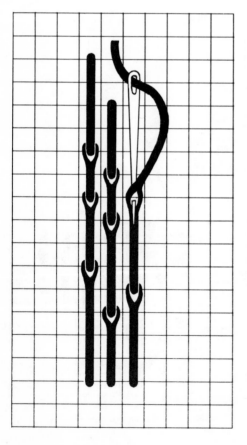

UPRIGHT SPLIT GOBELIN STITCH — a fast-working stitch for textured accent or decorative backgrounds. Also good for shading because colors may be changed as often as necessary. This is not a hard-wearing stitch and it gives little coverage on the back of the canvas, but it's a great stitch for a heavy or thick surface look. Wool must be full or canvas will peek through. Easy and quick to do.

Work from either left or right side of area, but start each row at the bottom and work to the top of area.

To start, make first stitch up over 6 horizontal threads and then needle under 1 thread, bringing needle up *through* the yarn at the top of the stitch, splitting it. Next, stitch up over 4 horizontal threads, needle under 1 thread and split top of stitch; continue up the row, working the stitches in random lengths over 3 to 8 threads. On next row, vary the length of the stitches so the split does not come on the same canvas thread as in the previous row (see diagram). *Don't* pull stitches tight.

WIDE GOBELIN STITCH — a large stitch similar to Slanting Gobelin stitch. Good for large areas, background, and filling, as well as for stripes. (See also Satin stitch, page 129.) Works fast.

Always work from left to right over 3, 4, or 5 horizontal threads and 2 vertical threads.

(end of Gobelin Stitches)

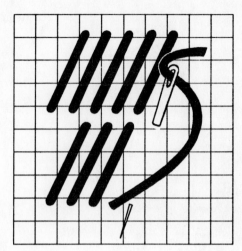

GREEK STITCH (Double Back stitch)

Greek stitch is a hard-wearing utility stitch, good for background, filling, and accents. It makes a close, pebblelike face and covers the back closely. This stitch is similar to Long-Armed Cross stitch (page 50) and Long-Legged Cross stitch (page 51); the difference is in the direction of the slant of the long arm. In this stitch, the slant alternates from right to left with each successive row. Be careful when working the stitch not to pull the yarn tight. Works fairly quickly.

Begin at left. Slant stitch *up to right* over 2 horizontal and vertical threads, bring needle up 2 meshes to left, slant next stitch *down to right* over 4 vertical and 2 horizontal threads, bring needle up 2 meshes to left, slant stitch *up to right* over 2 horizontal and vertical threads, and so on across area, ending with short stitch.

Return from right. Bring needle up 4 meshes below last stitch, slant stitch *up to left* over 2 horizontal and vertical threads, slant next stitch *down to left* over 2 horizontal and 4 vertical threads, and so on across area.

At back, needle is always horizontal under 2 vertical threads, alternating from the top to the bottom of the row.

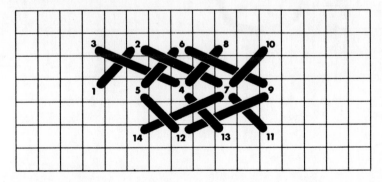

Stitch Guide		
	from	to
over	1	2
	3	4
	5	6
	2	7
	4	8
	6	
back	11	7
	9	12
	13	4
	7	14

HALF CROSS STITCH (see Basic Tent Stitch, page 28)

Herringbone Stitches

This small group employs slanted stitches worked so that the stitches slant alternately from left to right, then right to left.

CONTINENTAL HERRINGBONE STITCH (the return row is called Reverse Tent stitch; see below) — a small, firm utility stitch that is excellent for detail. (See also Kalem stitch, page 99, a vertical version of this stitch.) With just a bit of practice, this stitch works as fast and easily as the Continental stitch.

Work like Continental stitch (page 28) for first row. On return row, don't turn canvas — just change slant of needle, making the stitch slant in the opposite direction (that is, from lower right to upper left.)

Reverse Tent Stitch: This is the term used when referring to the return row *only* of the Continental Herringbone stitch. Reverse Tent stitch is seldom used alone. It is usually used in some combination with Tent stitch or other stitches to complete a variety stitch; it is also used for fill-in stitches.

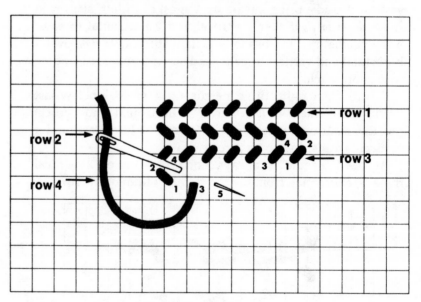

HERRINGBONE COUCHING STITCH — a combination stitch, medium to large in size, made with rows of Straight Gobelin stitch (page 89) tied down with a wide herringbone. For accents and special effects, as well as borders and stripes, this stitch can be most effective when worked in different plies of yarn, in different colors, or in wool couched with cotton floss, silk, or metallic threads. A decorative rather than a utility stitch (good for filling, but not background), it covers the canvas well but can snag if herringbone floats are too long. Works most easily one row at a time. Works up fast even though it takes two journeys to complete one row.

Work from the left. Lay in the Straight Gobelin stitch (shown here worked over 4 horizontal threads) and then work a herringbone over it (each stitch here is worked over 3 vertical and 4 horizontal threads, with the slant alternating to form the herringbone). Fasten off at end of row, and start next row at left — the herringbone does not work as a return row.

Note: Having two needles, one threaded in each yarn, is an advantage when working with two kinds of yarn.

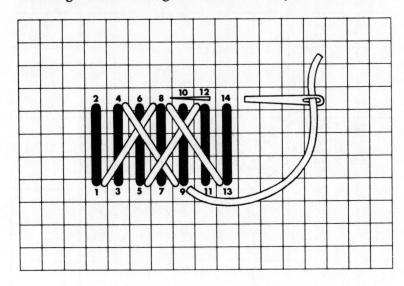

Stitch Guide

	from	to
first	1	2
journey	3	4
	5	6
	7	8
	9	
second	1	8
journey	4	9
	5	12
	8	

HERRINGBONE STITCH I (Fine Herringbone stitch, Witch stitch) — when worked over a 2 thread count, this is a small, close stitch, good for background and filling, that looks like a bias basket weave. On larger counts (over 4 or 6 meshes), the stitch is not so firm and is better used for decorative effects — it makes a braidlike stripe. When two or more colors are used, the stitch gives a zigzag effect. The stitches are close, so adjust thickness of wool to size of stitch, and take care not to split wool as you bring needle up from back. Don't pull stitches tight. The small stitch works up slowly; the larger the herringbone, the more quickly it works up.

This stitch *must* be worked from left to right. Slant stitch *down to right* over 2 horizontal and vertical threads, insert needle from *right to left* under 1 vertical thread, slant stitch *up to right* over 2 horizontal and vertical threads, insert needle from *right to left* under 1 vertical thread, and so on. At back, needle is always inserted horizontally from right to left, first at bottom, then at top of row. Start next row at left, 1 mesh below first stitch of completed row.

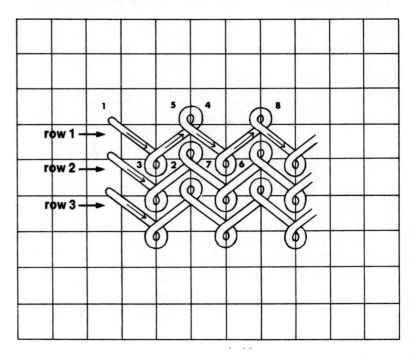

HERRINGBONE STITCH II (Herringbone-Gone-Wrong stitch) — similar to Herringbone stitch I, except it looks like a double basket weave and it can be worked over and back. Worked over a small count, this gives a very close, firm surface; worked over a larger count, it can be most decorative. Be careful not to split yarn as you bring needle up from back, and don't pull stitches tight or yarn may slip. The smaller stitch works slowly; the larger the herringbone, the more quickly it works up.

Row 1: Work from the left. Slant stitch *down to right* over 2 horizontal and vertical threads, insert needle from *right to left* under 1 vertical thread, slant next stitch *up to right* over 2 horizontal and vertical threads; continue to end.

Row 2: Work from the right (don't turn canvas). Starting 1 mesh below last row, slant stitch *down to left* over 2 horizontal and vertical threads, insert needle from *left to right* under 1 vertical thread, slant stitch *up to left* over 2 horizontal and vertical threads; continue to end.

Alternate rows over and back until entire area is filled.

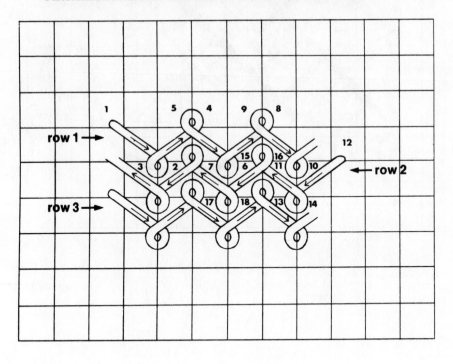

TWO-COLOR HERRINGBONE STITCH — a combination of yarns and colors makes this decorative stitch excellent for accenting and for special striped or border effects. It can also be used for filling, although this is not a utility stitch (there is very little coverage on the back to give durability). The stitch size can be varied, too — it can be worked over 3, 4, 5, or 6 threads. Works rather fast even though each row takes two journeys.

A herringbone stitch is worked, and then an identical herringbone, in a different color, is worked over it. Work from left to right, following Stitch Guide and diagram.

Stitch Guide

	from	to
color 1	1	2
	3	4
	5	6
	7	8
	9	
color 2	11	5
	12	7
	2	9
	4	13
	6	14
	8	

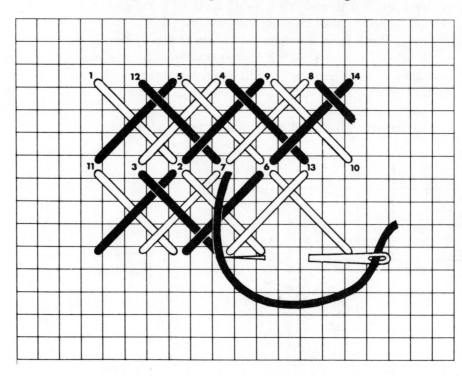

WIDE STRIPE HERRINGBONE STITCH — this makes an impressive and colorful stripe. A decorative stitch, it is excellent for borders, bands, and accents. Used as an allover repeat, it makes a pretty honeycomb pattern. Once started, the herringbone works quickly and easily, and is fun to do. Just take care and don't pull the stitches tight. It's easiest to work if the area is marked off — use a needlepoint marker to mark off 8 horizontal threads for each stripe. Work from the left.

Color 1: Bring needle up 2 meshes above bottom of stripe, carry yarn *down to right* over 2 vertical and horizontal threads, insert needle from *right to left* under 2 vertical threads, carry yarn *up to right* over 8 vertical and horizontal threads, insert needle from *right to left* under 2 vertical threads, carry yarn *down to right* over 8 vertical and horizontal threads. Continue alternating the stitch *down to right* and then *up to right* over 8 threads to end of area.

Color 2: Bring needle up 2 meshes above start of color 1. Carry stitch *down to right* over 4 vertical and horizontal threads, insert needle from *right to left* under 2 vertical threads and carry yarn *up to right* over 8 vertical and horizontal threads. Continue to end of area.

Following diagram, start **color 3** in second mesh above start of color 2 and start **color 4** in second mesh above start of color 3. **Color 5** and **color 6** are worked *up to right* and then *down to right*. Follow diagram and Stitch Guide. Colors 5 and 6 "square the corner" and then follow the pattern for the rest of the stripe. Be careful to keep the herringbone even at the beginning of each color row.

Stitch Guide		
	from	to
color 1	1	2
	3	4
	5	6
	7	8
	9	
color 2	10	11
	2	12
	4	13
	6	
color 3	14	15
	11	16
	12	17
	13	
color 4	18	19
	15	20
	16	21
	17	
color 5	10	22
	23	24
	19	25
	20	
color 6	1	5
	22	7
	24	9
	25	

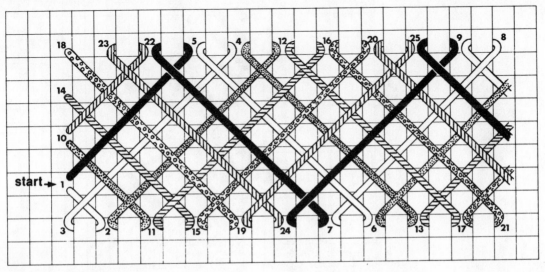

(end of Herringbone Stitches)

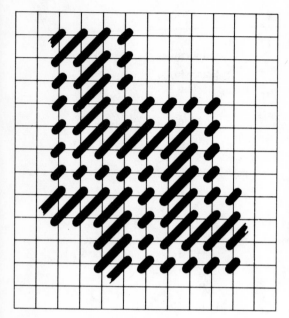

JACQUARD STITCH

This pretty utility stitch is good for large areas. It combines Continental stitch (page 28) and Slanting Gobelin stitch (page 89) in regular steps. Jacquard covers canvas well, making a firm, smooth surface. Don't pull stitches too tight because this stitch will pull crooked. Try it in two colors. Works quickly and easily once you get used to the count.

Usually worked from top left to bottom right, this stitch can also be worked from the bottom up. Start with a slanted stitch over 2 horizontal and vertical threads and work in steps of five stitches. Work five stitches across from left to right, then four stitches down, then four stitches across; continue to end of area. Work a row of Continental stitches in the same or a contrasting color before working the next row of slanted stitches. After area is completed, a few Tent stitches may be needed to fill in where "steps" have been broken by the design.

Steps may also be worked in units of six stitches; larger steps are not recommended because pattern loses its definition.

Variation: For a slightly different look, and to keep your canvas from pulling so crooked, try the stitch using the Reverse Tent stitch (see Continental Herringbone stitch, page 92) instead of the Continental stitch. It is just as pretty, and doesn't pull the canvas as much.

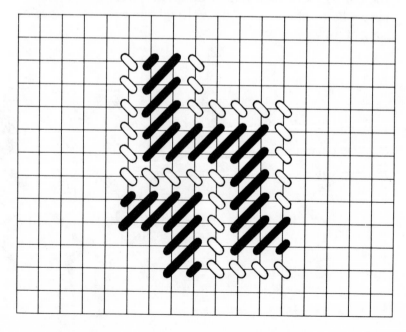

KALEM STITCH (Tapestry stitch)

A small, tight stitch, this is worked in vertical rows from right to left. (See also Continental Herringbone stitch, page 92, and Continental stitch variation, page 28.) An all-purpose utility stitch, it is especially good for texture and stripes. It can be worked effectively in two colors. Makes a firm, hard-wearing surface. Easy to do, and works fairly fast.

Start from the right. Work first row from top to bottom in Continental stitch variation. Work next row from bottom to top, to the left of the row just worked, reversing the slant of the stitch.

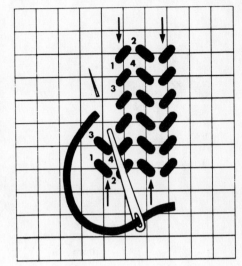

KNIT STITCH

Another small vertical stitch, Knit stitch resembles the stockinette stitch of hand knitting. Makes a firm, hard-wearing surface both front and back. This is a good utility stitch that is also effective in two colors. Similar to the Kalem stitch (above), it works a bit faster because it is a little larger.

Work over 2 horizontal threads and 1 vertical thread. Each stitch starts 1 mesh above (or below) last stitch. Work first row from bottom to top starting at right side of area; work next row from top to bottom, directly to left of row just completed. Continue in this manner.

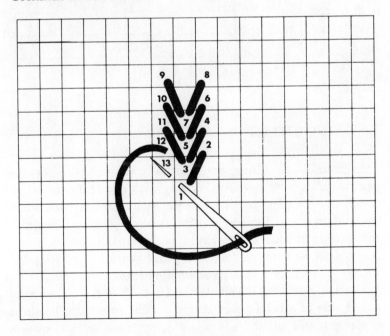

Stitch Guide

	from	to
up	1	2
	3	4
	5	6
	7	8
down	9	7
	10	5
	11	3
	12	1
	13	

KNIT-ON-THE-DIAGONAL STITCH

This is another version of the Knit stitch. Covers canvas well, but is better for special effects than for utilitarian purposes. Works fairly fast, but is easier to do on a frame than in-the-hand.

Work in diagonal rows. Start first row at lower left of area and work up to right. Work next row down to left, from top to bottom. Continue in this manner across area. "Up row" stitch slants *up to right* over 1 horizontal and 2 vertical threads; "down row" stitch slants *down to left* over 1 vertical and 2 horizontal threads. Do not pull stitches tight or yarn may slip and work will pull very crooked.

Stitch Guide

	from	to
up	1	2
	3	4
	5	6
down	7	6
	4	8
	2	9

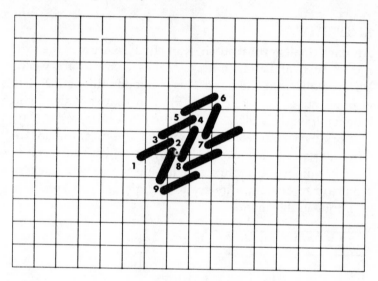

KNITTING STITCH (Railway stitch)

This small, tight utility stitch is useful for hard-wearing backgrounds and filling, and is usually worked on penelope canvas. (If worked on mono canvas, work over 2 threads as 1.) Stitch is finer when worked on penelope canvas than when worked on mono. Because this is a tight stitch, be sure wool is the proper thickness. Makes a very hard, strong surface. Similar to Knit stitch (page 99), but worked horizontally. Works more slowly than most small stitches.

Work in horizontal rows over and back, *bottom to top,* starting at left side of area. To start, bring needle up *between* 1 pair of horizontal (filling) threads. Slant stitch *down to right* over 2 double vertical threads. Continue to end of row. To return, bring needle up in mesh *above* double horizontal threads, slant stitch *down to left* over 2 double vertical threads, inserting needle *between* 1 pair of horizontal threads.

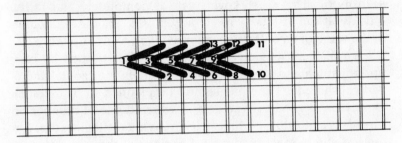

Stitch Guide

	from	to
over	1	2
	3	4
	5	6
	7	8
	9	10
back	11	9
	12	7
	13	

KNOTTED STITCH (Persian Cross stitch)

This is a small, slanting stitch, tied down in the middle by a single stitch. A good utility stitch, it makes a very firm, slightly nubby, hard-wearing surface with good, even coverage on the back. Can also be used for a texture accent. Easy to do and works fast.

Work in horizontal rows from left to right, top to bottom. Slant stitch *up to right* over 3 horizontal threads and 1 vertical thread, then work the hold (knot) stitch from *right to left* over the slanted stitch and the center thread intersection under the stitch. Two thrusts of the needle complete each stitch. Each row encroaches the last.

This stitch may also be worked over 5 horizontal threads.

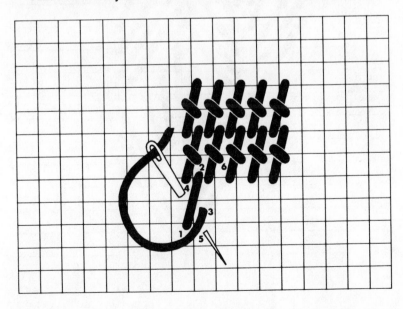

LEAF STITCH

This decorative flat stitch is excellent as a single motif and also effective for larger areas, even backgrounds. It is not a hard-wearing stitch, though, because of the length of the floats in each motif. This stitch covers canvas completely and fairly quickly. It can also be worked on top of finished needlepoint in the same or a contrasting color to give accent or texture.

Each leaf consists of ten slanting stitches topped by one upright stitch and is worked over a total of 9 horizontal and 6 vertical threads. The units should be planned to fit the area exactly or worked over an area in which the total number of threads is a multiple of three. Each individual stitch, except for the top stitch, is worked over 4 horizontal threads. The top stitch is worked over 3 horizontal threads. (The number of vertical threads varies — follow the diagram.) Work each leaf from the bottom, starting at the center and working to the outside edge. Work up the left side to the top and then down the right side to the bottom. A long Back stitch may be used as the center rib of the leaf, if desired. When used as grounding, work in horizontal, encroaching rows.

Stitch Guide

from	to
1	2
3	4
5	6
7	8
9	10
11	12
9	13
7	14
5	15
3	16
1	17

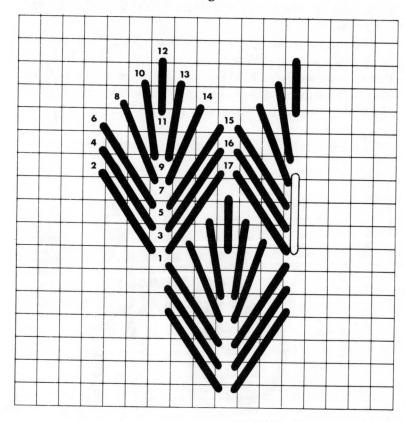

Variation: The stitch is worked over 10 horizontal and vertical threads, so it is diamond-shaped. This variation is sometimes better in bolder or more modern designs than the smaller, traditional leaf-shaped unit.

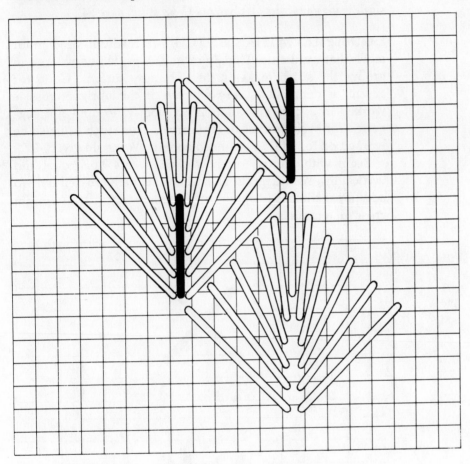

Leviathan Stitches

All Leviathan stitches are really Cross stitches, but they are grouped separately here because they are most often used for special effects or as single motif units. (See also Smyrna Cross stitch, page 54.)

DOUBLE LEVIATHAN STITCH — a medium-sized motif stitch that can be used singly or in groups. When worked in groups the stitch makes a thick, bumpy surface. Good for accent or detail, it is very effective if the upright cross is worked in a different color. It's a wool-eater, and not suggested for backgrounds or large areas. This stitch can also be worked on top of finished needlepoint. Works slowly.

Begin with a cross stitch worked over 4 horizontal and vertical threads (diagram **a**). Each arm is then crossed by two additional stitches (diagram **b**). To finish, top with an upright cross (diagram **c**).

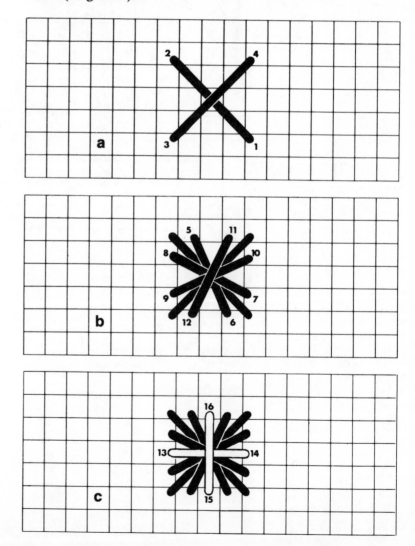

TRIPLE LEVIATHAN STITCH — a pretty, large motif stitch best used singly or in small groups. This is a tight, bumpy stitch; it is most effective in two colors. It can also be worked on top of finished needlepoint in the same or contrasting colors to give accent or texture. Works slowly.

Work the first section as an eyelet stitch, over 4 horizontal and vertical threads. Work from the outside of the unit *into* the center mesh. (For even, smooth work, the needle is always worked into the center mesh in eyelet stitches.) Each of the four arms of the unit has three stitches slanted into the center. The first stitch is slanted over 1 vertical and 2 horizontal threads, the second is slanted over 2 vertical and horizontal threads, and the third is slanted over 2 vertical threads and 1 horizontal thread. This makes one arm. Continue working around the center mesh to complete the arms (diagram **a**).

Finish the motif with five Upright Cross stitches (page 61), each made over 2 vertical and horizontal threads positioned between the arms at the top, bottom, each side, and center (diagram **b**). Be sure all top stitches of the crosses lie in the same direction (that is, either all horizontal or all vertical).

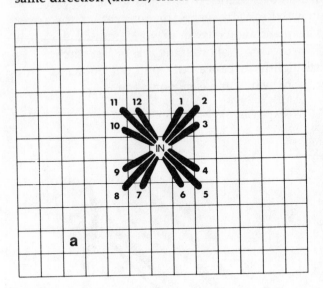

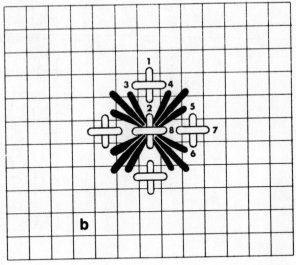

(end of Leviathan Stitches)

MILANESE STITCH

Milanese stitch is an old stitch that shows up nicely in a large area. Good for background, filling, and accenting textures. It covers the face of the canvas well, but is subject to snags because of the long floats in each unit. This is a great wool-user, but works fairly quickly.

Individual rows of slanting stitches form triangular units of four slanting stitches. The units form a diagonal pattern that alternates in direction — every other row of triangular units points in the same direction (see diagram).

Row 1: Back stitch over 4 thread intersections, then over 1 intersection, again over 4 intersections, and so on. Repeat to end of area.

Row 2: Start 1 mesh below first row. Back stitch over 3 thread intersections, then over 2, over 3 again, and so on. Repeat to end of area.

Row 3: Start 1 mesh below second row. Back stitch over 2 intersections, then over 3, then over 2, and so on. Repeat to end of area.

Row 4: Start 1 mesh below third row. Back stitch over 1 intersection, then over 4, then over 1, and so on. Repeat.

Start again with Row 1, repeating the four pattern rows over the area. To keep a straight edge or to work around a design, it is sometimes necessary to shorten the first or last stitch.

Don't work tightly or canvas will pull out of shape. This stitch works more evenly and easily on a frame.

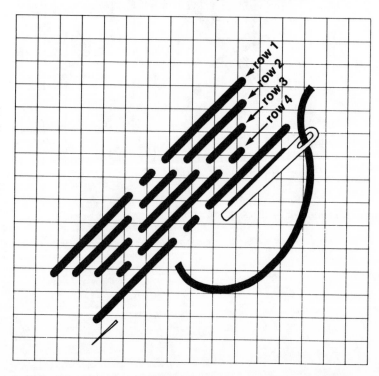

Variation: Triangular units of four flat stitches worked in diagonal rows will give the same effect, and this variation uses less yarn because of the shorter stitches on the back. Works up fairly quickly.

Each unit of four stitches begins with a stitch over 1 thread intersection, then a stitch over 2 intersections, then over 3, then over 4; repeat stitch unit to end of area. Work length of entire diagonal row, from top left to bottom right, then return from bottom to top (don't turn canvas). Each row is worked under and fits into a completed row, with the direction of the triangular units reversed. Again, to keep a straight edge, it is sometimes necessary to shorten some of the stitches (see diagram below).

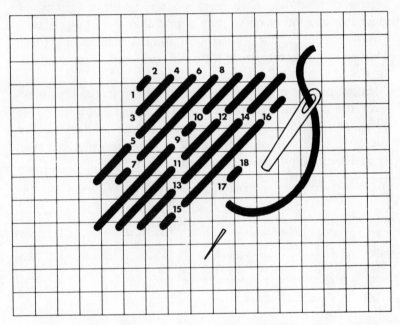

Mosaic Stitches

The basic stitch unit for this group consists of three stitches that slant to the right: the first a Continental stitch (page 28), the second a slanting stitch, and the third another Tent stitch. These are small, firm utility stitches for general use and hard wear. Also good for decorative effects. Variations may be worked by reversing the slant of the stitches for alternating rows or by alternating the slant of the stitches in the units of a row.

DIAGONAL MOSAIC STITCH — an all-purpose utility and decorative stitch that works up quickly.

Starting at the right side of the area and working toward the left, work rows diagonally from top left to bottom right. Stitch over 1 thread intersection, then over 2, then over 1 again; with needle vertical under 2 horizontal threads, start the next unit — over 1 intersection, over 2, over 1 again and so on to end of area.

Some people prefer to work each row from the top; however, the stitch can be worked down and *then* up (similar to the Diagonal Tent or Basket Weave stitch, page 29) if desired. The face will look the same; the back will be irregular but well covered, and it will not pull so crooked.

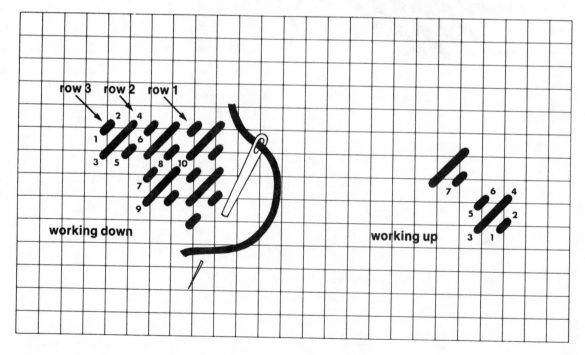

HORIZONTAL MOSAIC STITCH — here, the basic Mosaic unit of three stitches is worked in horizontal rows over 2 horizontal threads. Back coverage is smooth and full. This is a good utility stitch and it works fast.

Working from the top, start at the right side of area. Bring needle up under the 2 horizontal threads that will hold your first row. Make a Tent stitch over 1 thread intersection. The second stitch slants to the right over 2 intersections. The third stitch, over 1 intersection, completes the unit. Continue row across area. For return row, turn canvas and work back from right to left. The small square units are each made directly under the one of the row above.

Variation: A different method of working Horizontal Mosaic stitch is useful for large areas. It requires two journeys to complete, but works fast and keeps the canvas from pulling crooked because all the stitches on the back are straight.

In first journey, cover area with horizontal rows of slanted stitches worked from every other mesh over 2 threads. In second journey, fill in the small single stitches, working diagonal rows similar to Diagonal Tent or Basket Weave stitch (page 29). Follow diagram.

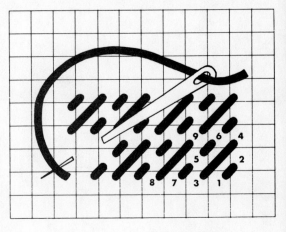

Stitch Guide

from	to
1	2
3	4
5	6
7	5
8	

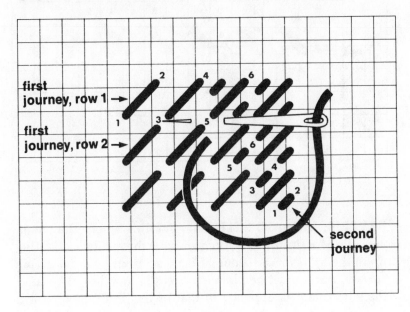

HUNGARIAN MOSAIC STITCH — with this stitch the basic Mosaic unit is worked in two journeys. Really a bit tedious to work, this stitch is best used for special areas or for working in two colors or in two yarn textures. Works slowly.

Work in horizontal rows across the canvas from top to bottom of area.

Row 1: Starting at the *right*, work a slanted stitch over 2 vertical and horizontal threads, work Continental stitch (page 28) over 1 intersection, slant needle under 3 vertical and 2 horizontal threads, slant next stitch up over 2 intersections, and continue across row. Don't pull stitches tight or canvas will pull quite crooked.

Row 2: Work back (don't turn canvas) from left to right, filling in the empty spaces with a small stitch slanting like the Tent stitch, to complete each Mosaic unit.

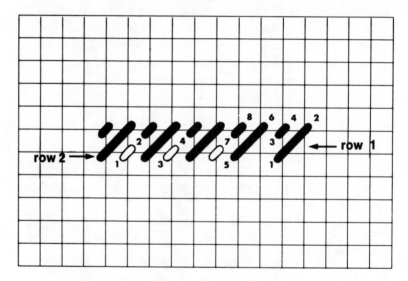

REVERSE MOSAIC STITCH — for this stitch, the small, versatile Mosaic unit is worked with the three stitches slanting up to the *left*. Worked alone, it makes a pretty, hard-wearing surface, but it must be planned carefully in a design because the stitch slant is opposite to that of the Tent stitch, and it doesn't always blend into other needlework as easily. Worked alternately with the Horizontal Mosaic stitch, it makes a pretty one- or two-color pattern. Works up easily, but not quite so quickly as the Horizontal Mosaic stitch.

To work this stitch alone, start at top right of area and work in diagonal rows to bottom left, from right to left of area (diagram **a**).

When alternating with the Horizontal Mosaic stitch (diagram **b**), work in horizontal rows from right to left.

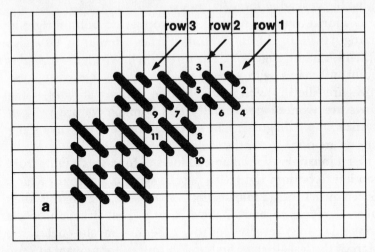 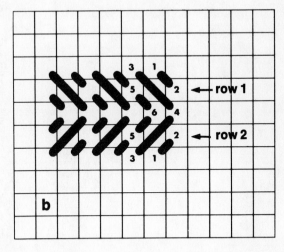

(end of Mosaic Stitches)

NORWICH STITCH (Southern Cross stitch)

A striking, square-on-square motif stitch that has a woven look and gives a dimensional quality to the surface, this is purely a decorative stitch, not a utility stitch. It makes a pretty border or allover pattern, especially when worked in alternating (two or more) colors. Interesting effects are created when the motifs are used in small groupings. Gives full coverage of canvas on the face, but very uneven coverage on the back. Be careful not to pull the stitches tight. Works slowly.

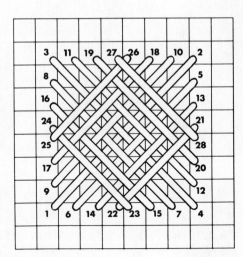

A fairly large stitch, it can be worked in various sizes — just be sure that the area to be worked has an *uneven* number of threads (for example, 7 horizontal threads and 7 vertical threads). Mark off the square area to be worked, using a needlepoint marker. Work *around* the area, crossing the face diagonally with long stitches. The first and second stitches cross the area diagonally from corner to corner. Succeeding stitches alternate crossing the face of the square, making a raised, woven, diamond-shaped pattern in the center of the square area.

Follow the diagram — bringing the needle *up* in the *uneven* numbered meshes on the diagram, *down* in the *even* numbered meshes — until you get the plan of the pattern.

ORIENTAL STITCH

This is a fairly large stitch, good for background and filling, that is related to the Scotch stitch (page 135). Pretty when worked in two shades. Covers canvas quickly even though it must be worked in three journeys.

Diagonal rows are worked from top left to bottom right in triangular units of four slanting stitches (similar to Milanese stitch variation, page 107). The direction in which the triangles point alternates with each row. The spaces between these rows are filled in with units of three slanting stitches; some rows are worked horizontally and some rows are worked vertically (see diagram). The stitch can be very effective if the fill-ins are done in another color.

First journey: Work diagonal rows of four-stitch units from top left to bottom right. (It's best to start in a corner.) *Row 1:* Stitch over 1 thread intersection, next over 2, then over 3, then over 4; repeat to end of area. *Row 2:* The direction of the triangular units reverses for row 2. Begin 4 meshes below the start of the last stitch of first unit of row 1. If you want to keep the edge even, the first two stitches of the first unit must be *shortened,* so slant stitch up over 2 intersections three times, then over 1 intersection, making a partial unit. Continue down row, repeating full units — over 4 intersections, over 3, over 2, then over 1 — to end of area. As you practice the stitch, you will learn how to adjust the pattern and use a partial unit to keep a straight edge or to work around a design.

Second journey: Work horizontal rows of slanting fill-in stitches from left to right across canvas, and from *top to bottom* of area. Each stitch is worked over 2 thread intersections; each unit consists of three stitches.

Third journey: The vertical rows of fill-in stitches also slant up to the right. These three-stitch units are worked from right to left and from *bottom to top* of area. Like the horizontal stitches, each is worked over 2 thread intersections.

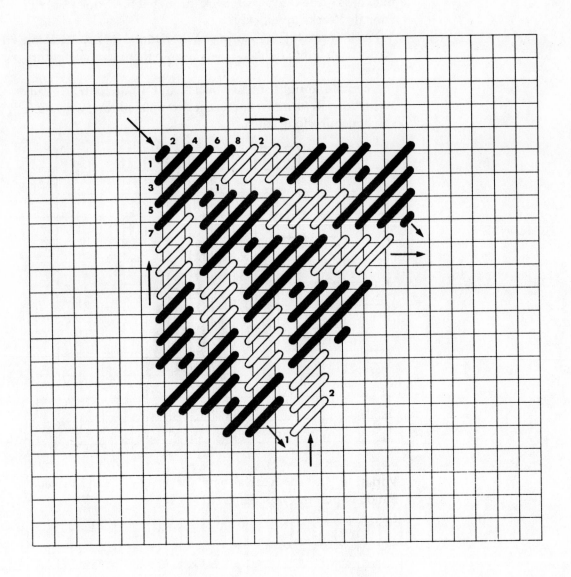

PARISIAN STITCH

Parisian stitch is a small, upright utility stitch. Check wool thickness — the canvas will peek through if the wool is not full enough. Works up quickly.

Work from top of canvas in horizontal rows, stitching across from left to right and back from right to left (do not turn canvas).

Alternate upright stitches over 2 and 4 horizontal threads across row. Return row encroaches completed row, with short stitch meeting long stitch.

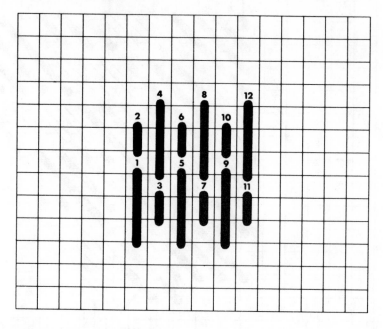

Variation: This stitch can also be worked over 1 and 3 threads, but don't pull the yarn tight!

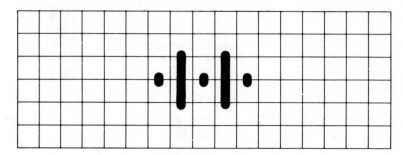

PLAIT STITCH (Spanish stitch)

Here, another stitch with a herringbone look, but it is worked more like a cross stitch. Excellent for bands and stripes. Makes a slightly raised, braidlike row on the front and gives smooth, even coverage on the back. Works quickly.

Work rows across the area from *left to right*. Slant stitches alternately, first to right and then to left, over 2 vertical and 3 horizontal threads. Can be worked over 2 or 4 horizontal threads as well. Needle is always vertical at the back.

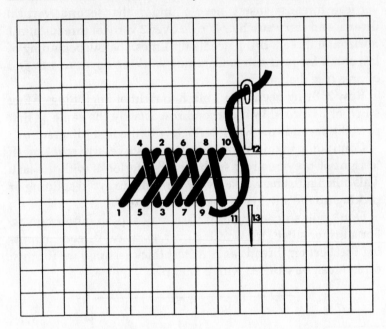

Stitch Guide

from	to
1	2
3	4
5	6
7	2
3	8
9	6
7	

PLAITED STITCH

Small and intricate, this stitch is similar to the Fern stitch (page 74). Good for filling, texture accents, and small areas, but tedious to work in large areas like backgrounds of large pieces. Two or three colors give an interesting effect. Works slowly.

Work in vertical rows across 3 vertical threads, starting at top left.

Row 1: Slant stitch *down to right* over 1 horizontal and 2 vertical threads, insert needle under the second vertical thread, and carry stitch *up to right* over 2 vertical threads and 1 horizontal thread. Bring needle up 1 mesh below beginning of last stitch for next stitch. Continue working down row to end of area (see diagram **a**).

Row 2: Bring needle up 1 mesh to right of beginning of first stitch of first row. Work second row exactly the same as first row; the second row will interlock with the first (diagram **b**).

Continuing in this manner, start each successive row 1 mesh to right of previous row so that each interlocks with the last. This stitch must be worked very carefully to avoid splitting or picking up the stitches of the preceding row.

Don't pull stitches tight or yarn may slip on mono canvas. For a firmer stitch, try working over 4 vertical threads, counting the 2 center threads as 1. Adjust thickness of yarn for this; often it can be worked with a finer ply.

Stitch Guide

from	to	
1	2	around thread
3	4	
5	6	around thread
7	8	
9		

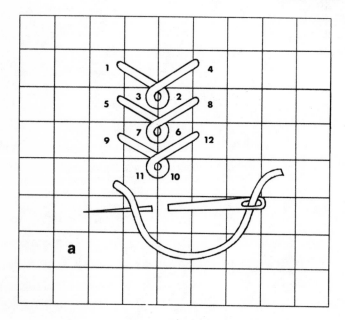

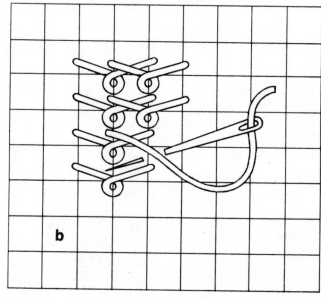

PLAITED EDGING STITCH

Plaited Edging stitch gives a piece of work a practical, strong, and pretty finished edge of smooth, small cross stitches. Originally used for rugs, but now being used more and more for accessories, wall hangings, and special pieces. A heavy wool-user, but worth it for the good finish. Two-ply wool usually works best for accessory and other small items; for rugs, a full strand of rug yarn is usually used. Works quickly.

For small pieces it is best to work piece and block it, *then* work the plaited edge. (It is very difficult to block needlepoint after the edge has been finished.) Prepare edge by turning unworked canvas toward back, the meshes matching, leaving 2 canvas threads along the top edge. Baste in position with sewing thread, mitering the corners as you come to them. The edges of the entire piece should be turned back and basted before the edging stitch is begun. Excess canvas may be trimmed to ⅝ inch. The last stitch of the needlepoint and the edging stitch always share a mesh.

Work the edging stitch from *right to left* along folded edge. Needle is *always* inserted from the back to the front. Bring needle through mesh directly below fold, at right side of edge being worked. Carry yarn up and over edge *and* tag end into the next mesh to the left (diagram **a**), then back to the right through the mesh you started in. This anchors the yarn. Now carry the yarn over the edge, bringing needle through from the back 3 meshes to the left of starting mesh, then over the edge, bringing the needle through from the back 2 meshes to the right. Continue, always carrying the yarn over the edge, 3 meshes to left, then back 2 meshes to right. A neat row of cross stitches will cover the folded canvas edge.

Stitch Guide

from	to
1 over edge	2 over edge to right
1 over edge to left	4 over edge to right
2 over edge to left	5 over edge to right
3 over edge to left	6 over edge to right

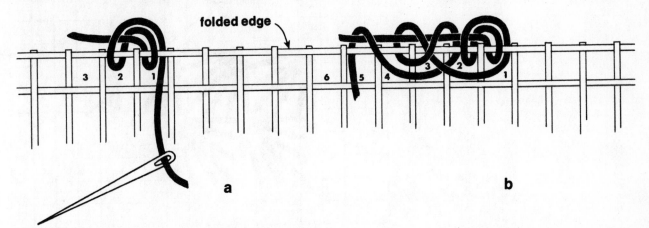

folded edge

a

b

RAY STITCH (Fan stitch)

A pretty background, filling, or accent stitch, this can be worked in a variety of ways for pattern effects. It's not generally used as a utility stitch because it snags easily. The rows of Ray units may be worked so the slant of the stitches alternates from the left in one row and from the right in the next row, or groups of units may be worked so the slant alternates from unit to unit. Also, the Continental stitch (page 28) can be combined with the small Ray units. Another interesting effect can be achieved by using two or more colors. Wool should not be too full for this stitch so the pattern can show. Works slowly.

It is easiest to work this stitch in horizontal rows. The unit is usually worked over 3 horizontal and vertical threads, with seven stitches in each unit, although it may be worked over a larger count with the necessary stitches added to complete the unit. Rows may be worked either to the left or to the right.

Starting at the lower left, work each stitch from the outside of the unit *into* the corner mesh. (For smooth, even work, when several stitches radiate from the same mesh, always work from the outside of the unit *into* that mesh.) Begin with one upright stitch over 3 horizontal threads. Following the diagram, work counterclockwise around the unit to the seventh, or horizontal, stitch. Complete each unit before going on to the next. Bring needle up 3 meshes to right of first stitch to start next unit.

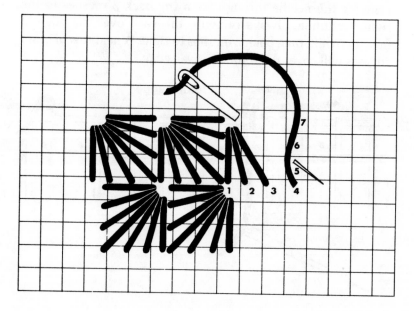

RENAISSANCE STITCH

This is a small, hard-wearing, tapestrylike stitch often used for upholstery. Stitch should completely cover canvas, so be sure that enough plies are used. This is a heavy wool-user. Works slowly.

Begin at top left of area and work the three-stitch unit from *left to right* in vertical rows. Bring needle up 3 meshes from the left and make a horizontal stitch over 2 threads to the left. From the mesh below (3), work an upright stitch over 2 threads, then make a second upright stitch from the mesh to right of the start of the last stitch, carrying it up over 2 horizontal threads *and* the horizontal stitch. Bring needle up 3 meshes below and 1 mesh to right and repeat three-stitch pattern. Continue to bottom of area. Start next row at top and work down.

Variation: This is a simplified version that also gives a hard-wearing surface, but not as tight a stitch. Yarn should be full so that canvas is completely covered. Works fast.

First lay Tramé (see Tramé stitch, page 144) between every other pair of horizontal threads. Then work Straight Gobelin stitch (page 89) over 2 horizontal threads *and* Tramé.

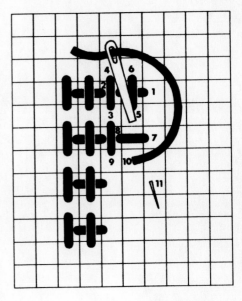

Stitch Guide

from	to
1	2
3	4
5	6
7	8
9	3
10	5
11	

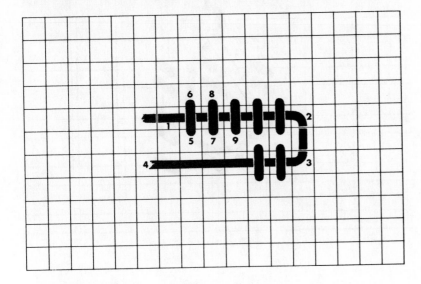

REP STITCH (Aubusson stitch)

This is another small, hard-wearing utility stitch developed from woven tapestries and rugs. Good for background, filling, and detail. When finished, the effect is a very fine rib like that seen in rep fabrics and old tapestries. This stitch should be worked on penelope canvas. Works slowly, but covers canvas completely. Start at right side of area.

Work in vertical rows from top to bottom. Slant stitches up to right, working over each *double* vertical thread as 1 thread, but using each *single* horizontal thread as 1 thread by pushing the 2 threads apart with your needle. For first stitch, come up *between* double horizontal threads, slant stitch up to right and go in *over* the double vertical threads, bringing needle up *below* double horizontal threads. For second stitch, slant stitch up over the double vertical threads and insert needle *between* double horizontal threads (follow the diagram).

If Rep stitch is worked on mono canvas, it must be worked over 2 vertical threads and 1 horizontal thread. The stitch is not as small as it is on penelope canvas.

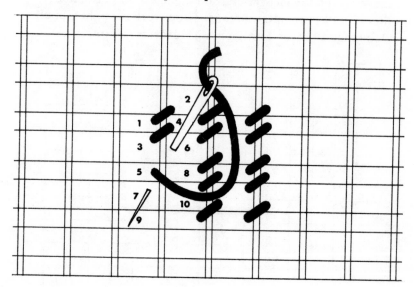

REVERSED EYELET STITCH

This motif stitch is pretty alone or when used in groups. It is tedious to work as a grounding unless you're working on a frame. Each motif comprises four corner units, each containing two straight and five slanted stitches. If working in combination with other stitches, be sure to count threads and mark area so units will fit space. Works slowly.

Bring needle up in mesh that will be center of motif (mesh 1) and make a Tent stitch. Bring needle up 1 mesh to right of center and slant stitch *up to right* over 1 vertical and 2 horizontal threads. Bring needle up 1 mesh above center and slant stitch to right over 1 horizontal and 2 vertical threads. Bring needle up in second mesh to right of mesh 1 and slant stitch *up to right* over 1 vertical and 3 horizontal threads. Bring needle up in third mesh to right of mesh 1 and make a straight upright stitch over 3 horizontal threads. Bring needle up in second mesh above center and slant stitch to right over 1 horizontal and 3 vertical threads. Bring needle up in third mesh above center and make a straight horizontal stitch *to right* over 3 vertical threads. This completes one corner. Bring needle up in mesh 1 and continue around center to work the other three corners. Straight stitches or Back stitches may be worked between units in the same or contrasting colors (or yarns).

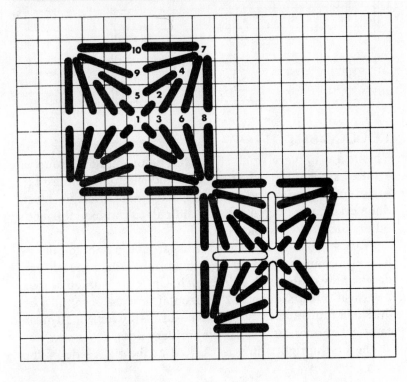

Stitch Guide

from	to
1	2
3	4
5	4
6	7
8	7
9	7
10	7
1	to next corner

REVERSE HALF CROSS STITCH (Lazy Knit stitch)

A small utility stitch worked on penelope canvas, this stitch gives a fine, horizontal herringbone effect. (On mono canvas, use the Continental Herringbone stitch, page 92, for a similar effect.) Works fairly fast.

Work from left to right in Half Cross stitch (page 30); work return row from right to left, reversing slant of stitches (no need to turn canvas).

Stitch Guide		
	from	to
over	1	2
	3	4
	5	6
	7	8
back	9	7
	10	5
	11	

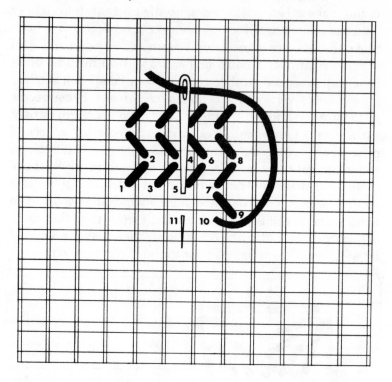

ROCOCO STITCH I

This is a very, very small stitch that belongs to the group of knotted stitches (French stitch, Knotted stitch). Often used in early embroideries and samplers, it is most effective when done on a fairly open mesh. It's difficult to combine this with other stitches. Works slowly.

Work stitch units in diagonal rows from top right to bottom left. Each unit is made up of four upright stitches, each tied down at the center with a tiny stitch. Units are worked *between* 2 vertical threads and *over* 2 horizontal threads. Yarn must be thin to fit four stitches into 1 mesh — use 1-ply for 8 or 10 mesh canvas. For finer canvas, use embroidery floss.

The first upright stitch is worked at the right side of the

mesh. The tie stitch is worked over both the upright stitch and the vertical thread (from mesh 3 to mesh 4). Work the next three upright stitches to the left of the first stitch and over the same mesh. Work tie stitches over the second and third stitches. Work the last tie stitch over the vertical thread as well as the last upright stitch (from mesh 4 to mesh 5).

To begin second unit, work first upright stitch from mesh 6 to mesh 5 (see diagram **d**).

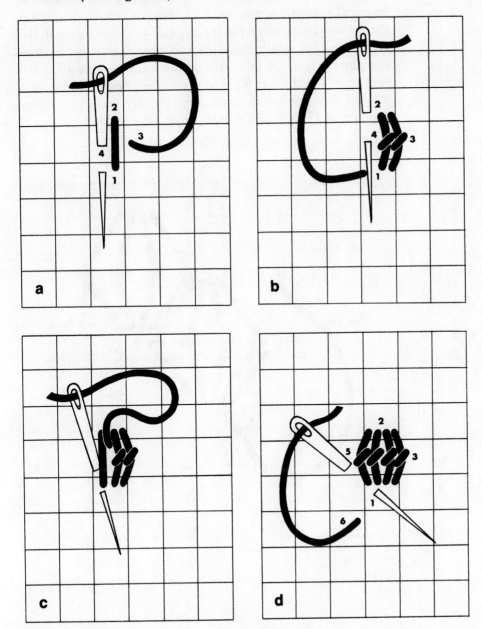

ROCOCO STITCH II

This is a larger and easier-to-work version of Rococo I. Makes a pretty, small pattern with a hard-wearing surface and good backing. Good for background, filling, and accent. Yarn should not be too full for this stitch — try 2-ply for 10 and 12 mesh canvas and 1-ply for 14 mesh canvas. Works slowly but fairly easily after a little practice.

Units of four tied-down upright stitches are worked in diagonal rows from top right to bottom left. Each upright stitch starts in the same mesh and ends 4 threads above in the same mesh. A small stitch worked over the center of each upright stitch ties it to a vertical thread, thus spreading the unit over 4 vertical threads at its center. Bring needle up 4 meshes below last tied-down stitch to start next unit. Follow diagram and Stitch Guide until you get the rhythm.

Stitch Guide		
	from	to
first unit	1	2
	3	4
	1	2
	4	5
	1	2
	5	6
	1	2
	6	7
second unit	8	7
	1	9
	8	7
	9	10
	8	

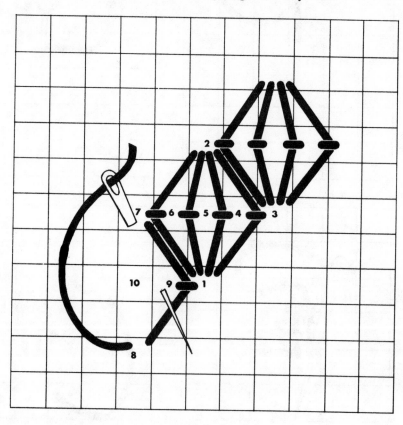

ROMAN STITCH (Roumanian stitch, Janina stitch)

Roman stitch is a versatile, pretty, knotted stitch that can be worked in various sizes, either horizontally or vertically. It can be hard-wearing or purely decorative, depending on the length of the stitch — the longer the stitch, the less wear it will give. Effective for background and filling, as well as border or stripe combinations. Works fast.

To work vertically, begin at top right side of area. Work a horizontal stitch from *left to right* over 4 vertical threads, bring needle up 2 meshes to the left, and make a small vertical (holding) stitch over horizontal stitch and thread. Continue, bringing needle up in mesh directly below start of first stitch and repeating horizontal and holding stitches to end of area. Start next row at top, to left of row just completed.

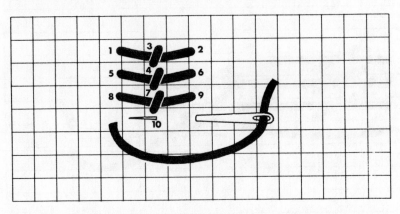

Stitch Guide	
from	to
1	2
3	4
5	6
4	7
8	9
7	

Variation: Alternate working horizontal stitches over 4 and 6 threads (two worked over 4 threads, then two worked over 6, for example). Tie down the horizontal stitch at its center with a small vertical stitch or with a slanted stitch worked over the horizontal stitch and 2 vertical threads. Works fairly quickly.

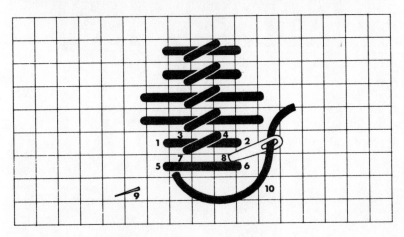

ROUMANIAN COUCHING STITCH

Basically, this is an embroidery stitch, but when adapted to canvas it becomes a decorative stitch (not a hard-wearing one) good for background, filling, and special effects. Works fast. (See also Tramé stitch, page 144.)

Work horizontally from left to right, from top of area down. Lay a long stitch along a horizontal thread and work back over it with evenly spaced holding stitches, each worked over 3 vertical threads. Yarn tension is important — the laid yarn should *not* be tight, but the holding stitches should be tighter so that the laid yarn will puff up between them.

Stitch Guide

from	to	
1	2	long stitch
3	4	
5	6	
7	8	
9		

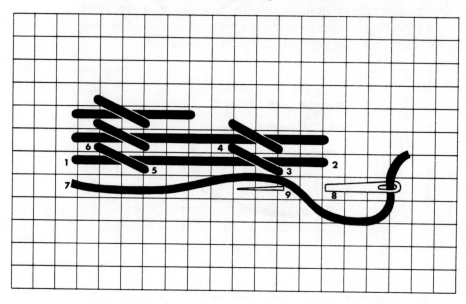

Satin Stitches

These are straight or slanted stitches worked evenly and close together to cover the surface of the canvas smoothly. Satin stitch can be worked in pattern areas; it can also be worked in rows for borders.

MOSAIC DIAMOND STITCH — an allover pattern of diamond-shaped units worked in horizontal rows, each row fitting into the preceding row. Nice for large areas, background, or filling. Wool should be full for complete coverage. Covers canvas quickly.

Each unit consists of upright stitches over 2, 4, 6, and 4 horizontal threads. Work across and back, left to right, right to left; the longest stitch of one row meets the shortest stitch of the next row. (If worked with slanted stitches, this would be Scotch stitch, page 135.)

For variation, 1 or 2 meshes may be skipped between rows of diamonds to be worked later in Tent stitch, Straight Gobelin stitch, or Slanting Gobelin stitch. Also, try working rows of diamonds from top to bottom with horizontal stitches. The stitch may be made larger, depending on the intended use — but the longer the stitch, the less hard wear it will give. This stitch can also be worked over 1, 3, 5, 7, 5, and 3 threads, but working over only 1 thread is always less firm than working over 2 threads.

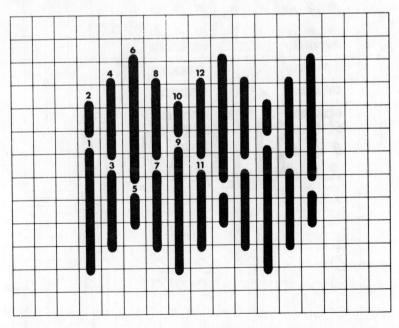

MOSAIC STAR STITCH (Mosaic Filling stitch) — a pretty combination stitch that makes an unusual background for a decorative piece or is effective as single motifs. Each unit consists of a center cross stitch banded by a square and surrounded by straight stitches. Pretty if worked in two colors. Works slowly.

To work an area, work units in horizontal rows. Adjacent units share straight stitches. Fill areas between Mosaic Star stitches with Tent, Cross, or Scotch stitches.

Work unit sections in the following order: straight stitches at top and sides, center square "box," center cross stitch. For the straight stitches, make four groups of four stitches over 3 horizontal or vertical threads, starting at the top of the unit and working counterclockwise (see diagram). Then bring needle up in lower right mesh (mesh 1) of center area (at top of last stitch of the bottom four stitches of the motif). Make center square "box" with four stitches — upright stitch at right side, straight stitch at bottom, straight at top, upright at left side. Bring needle up again in lower right mesh (1) of center area, and work cross stitch to finish center.

Stitch Guide

	from	to
box	1	2
	4	1
	3	2
	4	3
cross	1	3
	4	2

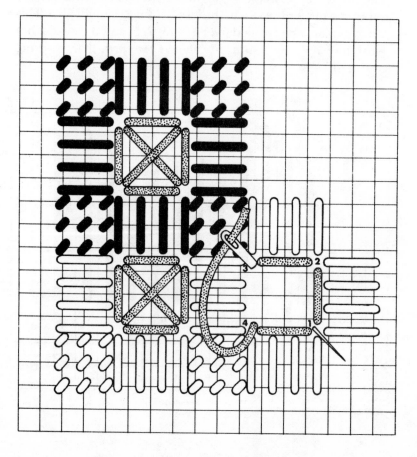

SATIN STITCH — a classic stitch of all needleworkers. (See also Straight Gobelin stitch, page 89, and Wide Gobelin stitch, page 91.) Wearing quality depends on the stitch size; the longer the stitch, the less wear the needlepoint will give. Used for background, filling, detail, and special effects. Works fast.

Even stitches, either straight or slanted, are made close together. Straight stitches may be worked either upright or horizontally over from 3 to 6 threads. Satin stitch may be worked from left to right or right to left.

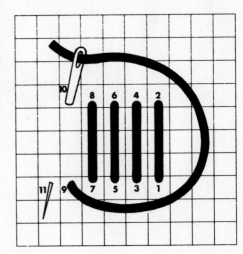

SATIN HERRINGBONE STITCH — a Satin stitch variation worked in vertical rows of slanting stitches. (See also Knit stitch, page 99.) Good for background and filling. Effective in two colors. Works fast.

Stitches are worked over 3 horizontal and 2 vertical threads, or stitch length may be varied by working over any count up to 6 horizontal and 6 vertical threads.

First row: Working from bottom up, slant stitch *up to right.*

Second row: Working from top down, slant stitch *down to right.*

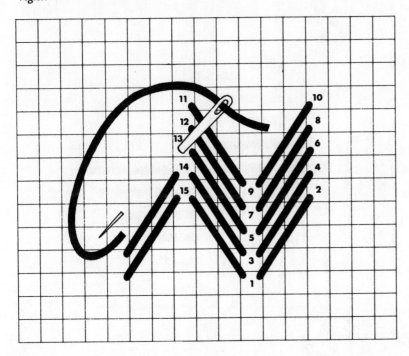

Stitch Guide

	from	to
up	1	2
	3	4
	5	6
	7	8
	9	10
down	11	9
	12	7
	13	5
	14	3

SATIN MOTIF STITCH — a diamond-shaped motif worked in Satin (or straight) stitches of graduating lengths. Usually used as single motifs, but interlocking rows make an impressive-looking texture stitch for large areas. Be sure yarn is full enough to cover canvas. Stitch works fast and easily, especially if you count off and mark canvas in advance to indicate area for each unit.

Working over an area of 12 threads by 12 threads for each unit, first work the upper right corner of the area. From the center mesh, make a straight stitch *up* over 6 horizontal threads. Then, working on to the right, next stitches are up over 5 threads, 4 threads, 3 threads, 2 threads, and 1 thread. Starting from the same center mesh, begin working lower left corner of diamond shape by making a straight stitch *down* over 6 horizontal threads. Then, working on to the left, go down over 5 threads, 4 threads, 3 threads, 2 threads, and 1 thread. The remaining two corners of the unit are worked in horizontal stitches, in the same or a different color, starting from the same center mesh. Work to left over 6 vertical threads, 5 threads, etc., and then from the center mesh to the right over 6 vertical threads, etc., ending at bottom of motif. Don't pull yarn tight, especially on stitches over 1 thread.

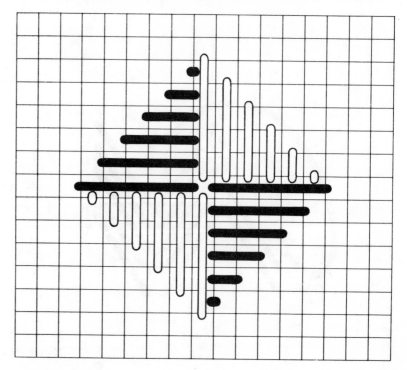

(end of Satin Stitches)

Scotch Stitches

There are several versions of the basic Scotch stitch; all cover the canvas completely, are excellent for large areas, are pretty, and work quickly and easily. (But be careful not to pull stitches too tight.) These stitches combine nicely with Tent, Gobelin, and Cross stitches.

CHEQUER STITCH (Checker stitch) — an old, often used general-use stitch made up of alternate units of Scotch and Tent stitches. Gives a textured surface and has good back coverage. Interesting when worked in two colors. Works up fairly fast.

Scotch stitch units may be made over from 3 to 6 vertical and horizontal threads. Work in diagonal rows starting at top left *or* bottom right. Fill in alternate squares with Tent stitch.

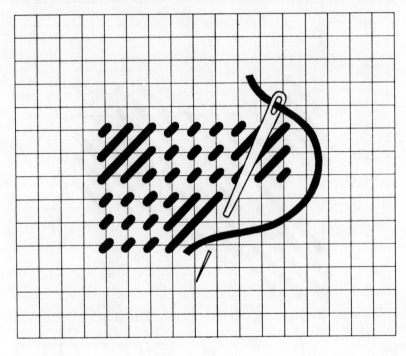

DIAGONAL STITCH — a large stitch that covers canvas well and is particularly useful for working large areas. Will pull out of shape if you work it too tightly. Works more evenly on a frame. Not classed as a utility stitch because the long floats can snag, but it is a stitch that wears quite well. Works fast.

Units may be worked over a count of from 4 to 8 vertical and horizontal threads. Work in diagonal rows from *top left* to *bottom right* or from *bottom right* to *top left* over, for example, 2, 3, 4, and 3 thread intersections, repeating to end of area. Next diagonal row fits into the pattern of the first row. Fill any spaces at canvas edges with Tent stitch or Slanting Gobelin stitch.

Back stitch in contrasting color and/or yarn may be worked between rows.

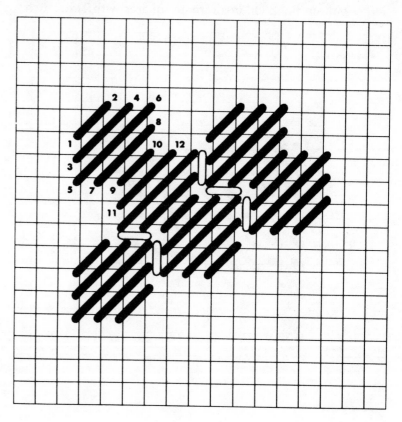

FLAT STITCH (Reverse Scotch stitch) — a name that is often used interchangeably with "Scotch stitch" in old descriptions of needlepoint; it is also used as a general descriptive term for many stitches. Used for background, filling, and area accent. Effective in two colors. Don't pull stitches too tight or canvas will pull out of shape. Works fast.

Flat stitch is made up of square units of slanting stitches (see Scotch stitch, page 135) in which every other unit slants in the *opposite* direction. Units may be worked over from 3 to 6 threads. Work in horizontal rows. Stitches of first unit slant to right, second unit slants to left, third to right, and so on. Work horizontal rows from right to left or left to right so that stitch directions of adjacent units alternate (see diagram).

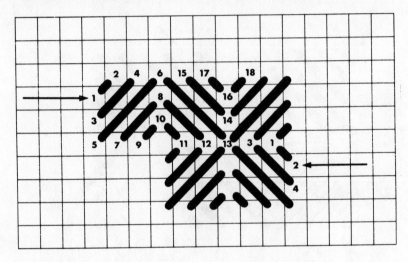

Stitch Guide		
	from	to
first	1	2
unit	3	4
	5	6
	7	8
	9	10
second	11	10
unit	12	8
	13	6
	14	15
	16	17
	16	18

Variation: Establish slant of stitches with first row and work subsequent rows so that the stitch directions are the *same*.

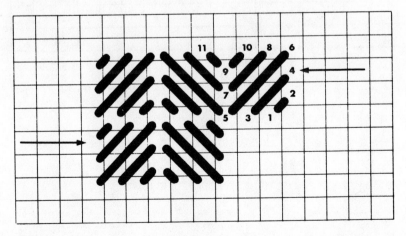

FLAT DIAGONAL STITCH — a very easy way to work Flat stitch (page 133) and really a "must" if working in two colors. Don't pull stitches tight. Covers a large area quickly.

Starting at top left, work down to right, slanting stitches to right over 1 intersection, over 2, 3, 4, 3, 2, 1, over 1 again, over 2, 3, and so on to the bottom of the area being worked. Stitches will form a diagonal row. Be sure to work two "over 1" stitches or the units will not be even (see diagram). For squares slanted to the left, start at top right and work down toward the left in the same manner as above.

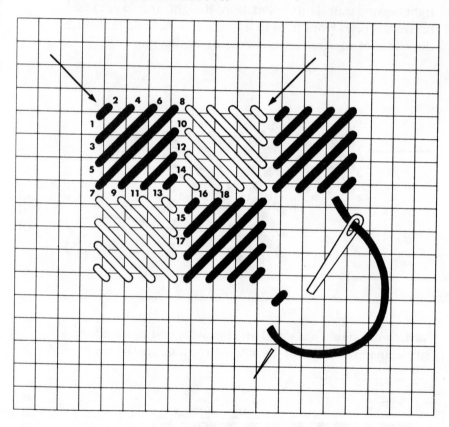

MOORISH STITCH — an old stitch used chiefly for large areas. Makes a pretty, puffy-looking surface. Both face and back of canvas are well covered. The smaller the stitch unit, the more hard-wearing the embroidery. Works quickly.

Stitch units may be worked over from 3 to 6 horizontal and vertical threads. Work a row of diagonal units and then a row of Tent stitch. (See also Jacquard stitch, page 98.)

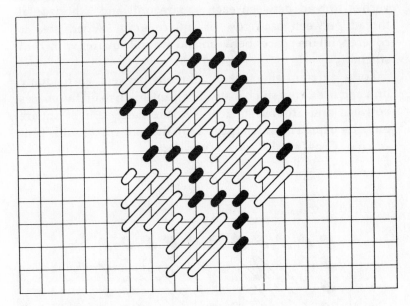

SCOTCH STITCH — an old stitch made up of square units of slanted stitches that give a soft, slightly puffy surface appearance. Scotch stitch is sometimes called Flat or Cushion stitch. It covers the canvas completely, and is excellent for large areas. It combines well with Tent, Gobelin, and Cross stitches. Works quickly and easily. One word of caution, though: Don't pull your stitches tight or the canvas will pull very crooked and in some cases start to pucker.

Work units in horizontal rows from left to right or right to left. Units may be made over from 3 to 6 horizontal and vertical threads. Starting at upper left of unit, work over 1 intersection (Tent stitch), then over 2 intersections, then 3, 4, 3, 2, and 1 to complete unit. Then bring needle up in mesh directly below top of longest stitch of unit just completed to start next unit in row (mesh 10 on diagram). Second row may be worked from right to left, starting 4 threads *below* last stitch. Work unit *up to left* over 1 intersection, then 2, 3, 4, 3, 2, and 1. Continue across row.

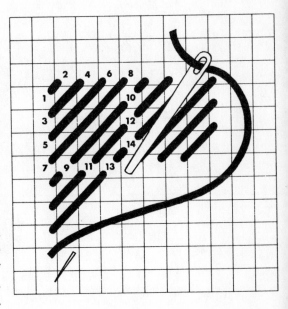

SCOTTISH STITCH (Large Square with Tent stitch, Quilted stitch) — an excellent general-use stitch combining the Scotch stitch with the Tent stitch. Two colors are most effective. Gives full coverage of canvas, with a surface texture that resembles quilting. Don't pull Scotch units too tight. Works quickly and easily.

Work the entire area in Scotch stitch (page 135), skipping 1 vertical thread between each square unit and 1 horizontal thread between each row of square units. When area is covered, fill the spaces between and around squares with Tent stitch.

For a different effect, skip 2 threads between each square unit and use Cross stitch instead of Tent stitch to fill the spaces between and around squares. Or alternate slant of square units by using Flat stitch (page 133); then fill spaces with Tent stitch or Cross stitch.

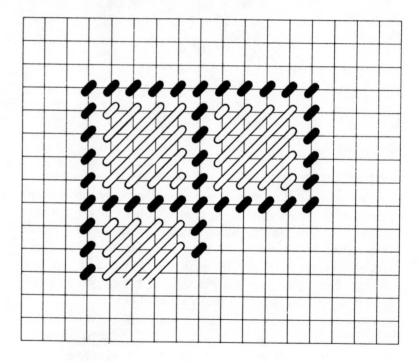

WOVEN STITCH — this version of the Scotch stitch is a general-use stitch that covers the canvas completely but works more slowly because it requires a second journey over the area. It is pretty in a large area, or it may be used to accent an area. Be careful not to pull stitches tight. Size of stitch may be made larger or smaller, depending on its use.

First, work an area in Scotch stitch (page 135). Then, using the same yarn or a novelty texture in a matching or sharply contrasting color, weave over and under the stitches (*not* through the canvas) of each square unit from corner to corner. For weaving, work in horizontal rows from right to left, weaving each stitch up from bottom right to top left (see diagram). Turn canvas for return row of weaving.

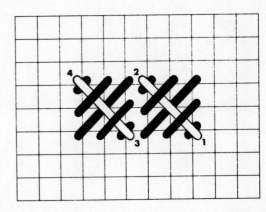

(end of Scotch Stitches)

SHEAF STITCH (Bundle stitch, Wheat stitch)

This old embroidery stitch works easily on canvas or it may be used for an interesting effect when worked over finished needlepoint. A sheaf may be used alone, spaced regularly or irregularly as accent, or may be worked in repeating rows to cover a large area. Size of sheaves is varied by number of upright stitches and the number of threads covered. Works easily and quickly both in-the-hand and on a frame.

Work in rows from *right to left*. Work three upright stitches over 4 horizontal threads (diagram **a**). Then bring needle up 2 meshes below top of last upright stitch and work a small horizontal stitch across the three upright stitches and 2 vertical canvas threads to form tie stitch, inserting needle 2 meshes below top of first upright stitch. Next sheaf begins in same mesh as last upright stitch of completed unit (see diagram **b**).

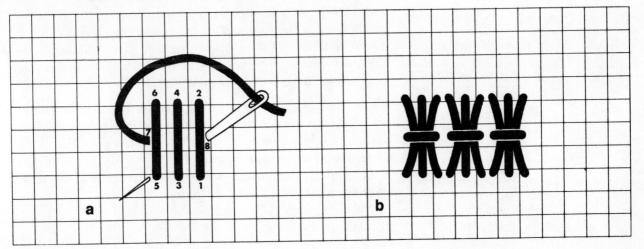

SHELL STITCH

This is a decorative stitch that covers face of canvas well, but not the back. Pretty when used as a border or accent banding, or as filling. Work in horizontal rows from right to left of area over 4 horizontal threads (may be worked over 6 threads also). A fairly complicated stitch that must be worked in two journeys. Works slowly.

First journey: Make units of four upright stitches, each unit held in the middle with a Back stitch. Bring needle up from back, carry yarn up over 4 horizontal threads and needle under 1 vertical thread into next mesh to left. (The vertical thread the needle goes under should be a "held-down" thread on mono canvas; see page 22.) Then carry yarn down over 4 horizontal threads, needle under 1 vertical thread into next mesh to left, carry yarn up over 4 horizontal threads, needle under 1 vertical thread to next mesh to left, and carry yarn down over 4 horizontal threads. This completes the four upright stitches. Now, bring needle up 2 meshes above and 1 mesh to right, at mesh 9 (see diagram **a**), and make a Back stitch over the four upright stitches and 1 vertical (center) thread to mesh 10 (see diagram **b**).

To start next unit, bring needle up in same mesh used by the bottom of last upright stitch (mesh 8). Continue working in horizontal rows until area is covered with these tied-in-the-middle units.

Second journey: Link the units by coiling the yarn one and a half times through the horizontal Back stitches (see diagram **c**). Don't pull these threaded-through stitches tight; they should loop up.

Another way to tie these units together is to work two journeys, using two colors (see diagram **d**). To start, use color 1 and thread yarn through Back stitches from the top, from the bottom, from the top, and so on across row. With color 2, alternate threading the yarn through the Back stitches to tie the units together. The looped stitch is pretty if worked in silk, cotton floss, perle cotton, or metallic yarn.

Note: The upright stitches of the first journey are sometimes made like the basic stitches of the Sheaf stitch (page 137). This makes a slightly bulkier stitch, but it is much easier if working in-the-hand rather than on a frame.

For variety, work a Cross stitch between each of the tied-in-the-middle units instead of looping the shells.

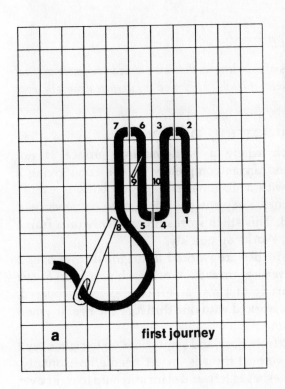

a — first journey

b

c — second journey

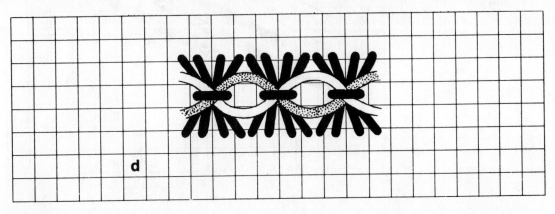

d

Slav Stitches

These are stitches of even lengths that are slanted over more vertical threads than horizontal threads. They give the surface a smooth, even look.

OBLIQUE SLAV STITCH, DIAGONAL — an excellent background stitch where a hard-wearing surface is not required. It covers canvas completely on the face, giving a smooth surface with a diagonal sweep; the back is evenly spaced small stitches. Keep stitches fairly loose or canvas will pull very crooked. This stitch works more evenly on a frame than in-the-hand. Works up quickly.

Long slanting stitches are worked in diagonal rows over 2 horizontal and 4 vertical threads. Work each row from *bottom left to top right*, starting first row at left of area to be covered. Each stitch can be worked with one thrust of the needle when working in-the-hand.

Bring needle up from back and slant stitch up to right over 2 horizontal and 4 vertical threads. Insert needle horizontally, bringing it out 2 meshes to left, and slant stitch up to right over 2 horizontal and 4 vertical threads. Continue in this manner until top of area is reached. New diagonal rows start at the bottom of the area being worked, 2 meshes to the right of first mesh of previous row.

Stitch Guide	from	to
row 1	1	2
	3	4
	5	6
row 2	7	8
	2	9
	4	10
row 3	11	12
	8	13
	9	14

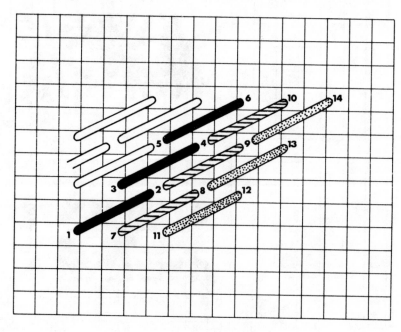

OBLIQUE SLAV STITCH, HORIZONTAL

OBLIQUE SLAV STITCH, HORIZONTAL — this stitch is similar to the diagonal Oblique Slav stitch, but it is worked in horizontal rows and has a little more coverage on the back. Don't turn the canvas while working this stitch; it will work up more easily and will give a smoother, more regular-looking surface if each row is worked from left to right. Be careful not to pull stitches tight or the canvas will become very lopsided. Works fast, especially on a frame.

Stitches are worked in horizontal rows, beginning at top of area to be covered. Working from left to right, slant first stitch up over 2 horizontal and 4 vertical threads. Bring needle up 2 meshes to right of beginning of first stitch, slant stitch up over 2 horizontal and 4 vertical threads, bring needle up 2 meshes to right of previous stitch, and continue in this manner until end of row. New horizontal rows start at left, 2 meshes *below* first mesh of previous row. When area is completed, fill in empty spaces at edges with Tent stitch.

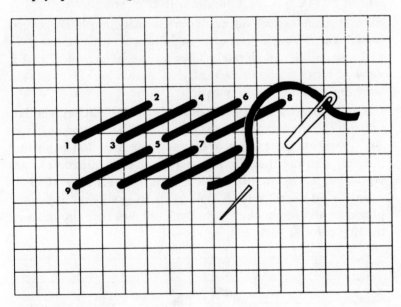

(end of Slav Stitches)

STAR STITCH

A small eyelet stitch, this is often used as a utility stitch as well as a decorative stitch — but only if time is no object! Pretty to look at, but slow to work in a large area. This stitch is similar to the Algerian Eye stitch (page 32) except here the yarn covers each 2 threads only once. Covers canvas fairly well. On large mesh canvas, Back stitch may be worked around each Star unit. Works slowly.

There are eight stitches to a unit. Starting at lower left of unit, alternate slanted and straight stitches, each over 2 threads, working from the outside of the unit *into* the center mesh. (For even, smooth work, the needle is always worked into the center mesh in eyelet stitches.) For a large area, it's easiest to work units in diagonal rows. Complete each Star stitch unit before going on to the next.

STEM STITCH (Long Oblique with Back stitch)

Stem stitch is a small, decorative stitch that completely covers the canvas, giving a pretty herringbone effect. Good for general use, filling, moderately large areas, or accent. Can be worked horizontally or vertically, as shown here. Not as fast working as some, but easy to do.

The Stem stitch is a combination of slanting stitches (similar to Satin Herringbone stitch, page 129) and Back stitches (page 34). Work alternate rows of slanting stitches, first from the bottom, slanting the stitch *up to right* over 2 horizontal and vertical threads, then down from the top, slanting stitches *down to right* over 2 threads. When slanting stitches are completed in an area, make single Back stitches (usually in contrasting color or yarn) between rows.

Stitch Guide

	from	to
up	1	2
	3	4
	5	6
	7	8
down	9	7
	10	5
	11	3
	12	1
Back stitch	3	1
	5	3
	7	5

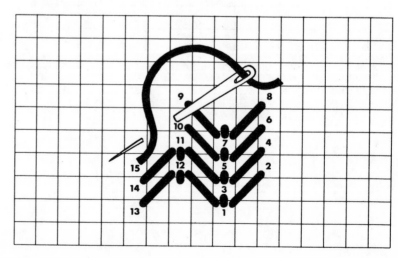

Tramé Stitches

In Tramé work, long stitches are laid along the filling (horizontal) threads of the canvas and then worked over with any of several stitches — usually Tent or Gobelin stitches. (See Trammed Cross stitch, page 57, for an example of Tramé worked with another stitch.) When working Tramé and stitch in the same yarn, the Tramé is usually laid on the canvas in the opposite direction to the direction of the stitch that is worked over it; when using different yarns, Tramé may be laid from right to left or left to right, whichever is easier for the stitcher.

Tramé is used to make a stitch appear fuller, to give depth of color, for decorative effect, for grounding, or to fill small areas. Novelty threads or yarns can be used for special effects; it can also be done in two colors. Worked with Gobelin stitches, it makes more of a ridge.

SPLIT TRAMÉ STITCH — a variation of the basic Tramé stitch, used when extra holding and smoothness are desired on mono canvas. If using thick yarn for Tramé for novelty and decorative effects, this method is a "must" so joining of stitches doesn't show. Work with care. Works easily but slowly.

Lay Tramé stitches along the horizontal threads from left to right (see Tramé stitch, page 144), but bring needle back around the last vertical thread of the stitch and split the yarn as the needle is brought up to begin a new Tramé stitch (see diagram).

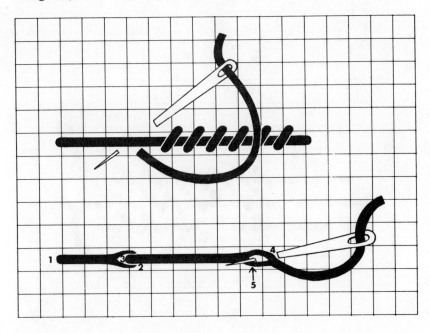

Stitch Guide

from	to	
1	2	around thread
split at 3	4	around thread
split at 5		

TRAMÉ STITCH — here, long stitches, laid along the horizontal threads of the canvas, are worked over with Tent stitches (page 28). Tramé can be done in two colors. Must be worked with care. Not a fast-working stitch.

Generally, Tramé works most easily on penelope canvas. Lay Tramé stitches first, working from right to left. Bring needle up between the double horizontal threads, lay the yarn along the horizontal threads to the left, and complete the Tramé stitch by inserting the needle in the center of a canvas intersection (see diagram). Then work over the Tramé with the Half Cross stitch (page 30).

On mono canvas, lay Tramé along a horizontal thread; pass needle under 1 vertical thread between each long Tramé stitch. (For extra holding, use the Split Tramé stitch, page 143.)

With both, vary the length of the Tramé stitches if covering a large area so joining will not show on the front of the canvas.

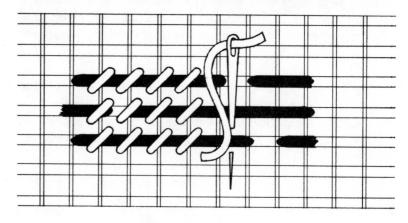

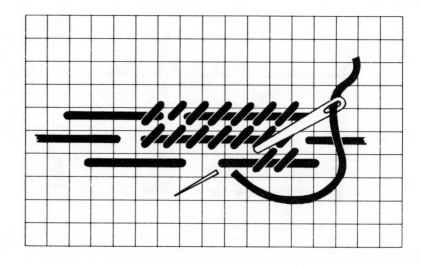

VERTICAL TRAMÉ STITCH — this is a pattern stitch suitable for an allover design, grounding, or any large decorative area. Striking and different effects can be obtained if two colors or two textures of yarn are used. Works slowly.

First, lay Tramé in area in a planned pattern. Now, work Tent stitch, Cross stitch, or Gobelin stitch over the Tramé in a regular pattern.

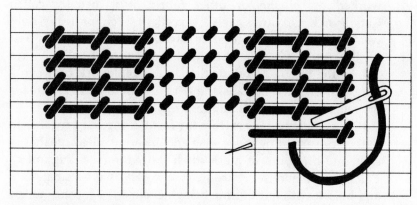

(end of Tramé Stitches)

TRIANGLE STITCH

This large, square stitch is very effective as a single motif or in groups. It also makes a most important-looking background for decorative pieces, but it is not a stitch for hard wear. Cross stitches are used in the corners. Works fast.

Work over a square of 8 horizontal and vertical threads. (A larger motif can be made by working over 10, 12, 14, or more threads, but thread count must be an even number.) To make working easier, mark off area with a needlepoint marker. Start working from top edge toward center of unit.

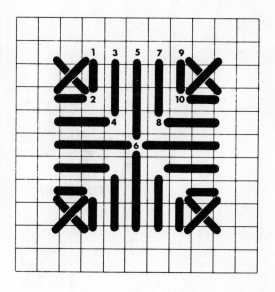

Bringing needle up 3 meshes from left (mesh 1), make a straight stitch down over 2 threads. The next stitch to the right is down over 3 threads, next stitch is down over 4 threads, then down over 3 threads, and finally down over 2. This makes the first of four triangular sections, all meeting in the center mesh. Work the next three sides in like manner. The square motif is now complete except for the corners; work a Cross stitch over 2 threads in each corner to complete motif.

For backgrounds, if using one color, it works best to complete each unit before going on to the next. A charming and most unusual effect can be achieved by working in two or three shades. Also good for use as corners with a border.

Tufted Stitches

These stitches are worked so the yarn may be cut on the surface to give a pile or a velvetlike effect. Stitches give a hard-wearing surface of loops if worked evenly but left uncut.

DOUBLE KNOTTED STITCH — an old stitch. When worked on muslin or other fabric, it is usually called Candlewick. On canvas, it is an excellent stitch for heavy-duty wear or for novelty decorative effect. Thick, full yarn is best for this stitch, which is a heavy wool-user. Works slowly.

Like the Single Knotted stitch, page 148, work between 2 double horizontal threads and over 2 double vertical threads on penelope canvas. On mono, work over 2 threads as 1.

Put needle into canvas from the front, bring out 2 meshes to left, carry yarn to right *under* tag end, insert needle 2 meshes to right and bring out in mesh stitch started in (see diagram **a**). Pull tight. Then reinsert needle *in same mesh*, make a small loop and hold it with left thumb; bring needle out 2 meshes to left (diagram **b**). Carry yarn to right *above* loop, put needle in 2 meshes to right, bring needle up again in starting mesh *between* small loop and "over" stitch (diagram **c**). Pull tight. Clip yarn and loop.

Complete each Double Knotted stitch and then work the next one.

Stitch Guide

from	to	
1	2	
3	1	
1	2	form loop
3	1	

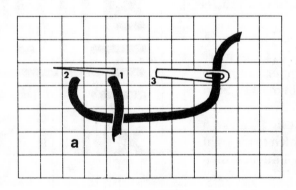

a

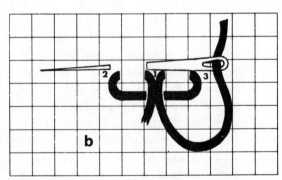

b

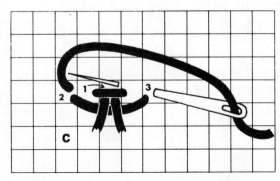

c

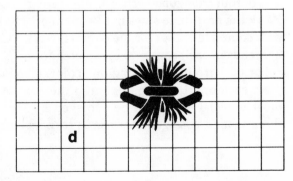

d

PLUSH STITCH (Berlin Plush stitch, Raised stitch) — a most popular pile stitch when raised work was *the* vogue during the Victorian period. Works best on penelope over 1 double thread intersection — or work over 2 threads on mono canvas. Good for grounding as well as filling, accents, and borders. A good rug stitch, but be sure your wool is full enough to achieve the pile effect. Loops may be left uncut if desired. This tight stitch holds well and works quickly. It's a great wool-user.

Work in horizontal rows from *left to right, bottom to top.* Bring needle up from back, carry yarn *up*, putting needle in mesh directly above starting mesh, and form a loop (diagram **a**). Then bring needle up again in starting mesh but to the left of the yarn already in that mesh, and hold loop with thumb. Make a slanting stitch (Half Cross stitch, page 30) over loop and 1 double thread intersection (or 2 threads on mono), and pull stitch tight (diagram **b**). This ties down loop and positions needle for next stitch. Bring needle out in mesh immediately below (diagram **c**), and continue working loop/slanting stitch units to end of row.

When area is completed, cut loops, trim, and fluff pile. (Take care loops are made evenly; this saves wool and makes the cutting and trimming easier. For a large area, loops may be worked over a guide.)

Stitch Guide

from	to	
1	2	loop
1	4	hold stitch
3	4	loop
3	6	hold stitch
5		

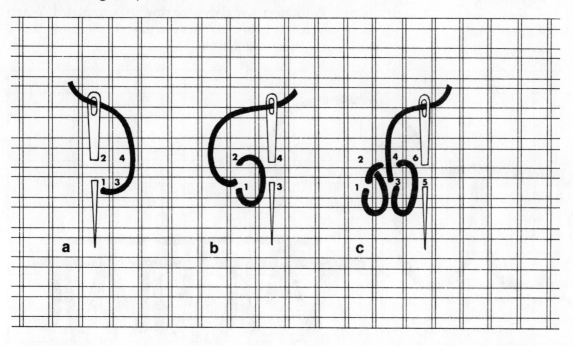

SINGLE KNOTTED STITCH (Turkey Knot stitch, Tufting stitch) — an old technique used on fabric as well as canvas to make a velvetlike surface, a soft pile, or when made with longer ends and loops, a fringe. Can be used for background, filling, and accent. Wool should be thick and *full* to make a tight stitch that will fluff up, and to keep the tufting from slipping. Works up fast and is interesting to do.

Work from *bottom to top* in rows across canvas from *left to right*. On penelope canvas each knot is made between 2 double horizontal threads and over 2 double vertical threads. On mono it's best to use 2 threads as 1. The needle is always inserted from the front to begin. Insert needle, then bring it up 2 meshes to left of starting point. Holding tag end down with thumb, carry yarn up to right over 4 vertical threads and insert needle 2 meshes to right of starting mesh, bringing needle up with one thrust in same mesh in which stitch started. Be sure the yarn comes out *under* the "over" stitch. Pull down hard to tighten stitch. Clip yarn.

In working an area, the yarn need not be clipped as each stitch is made. Work across the row from left to right, and as you make each stitch and tighten it, guide the length of the loop between stitches with your thumb (or work over a knitting needle or ruler) to get even loops to the end of the row. Now the row of tight stitches holding even loops is ready to be clipped. Work next row above the row just completed. When area is covered, trim to make an even pile. A soft brush can be used to straighten and fluff the pile.

Stitch Guide

from	to	
1	2	Yarn up and over to
3	1	Pull down tight.
4	3	Yarn up and over to
5	4	Pull down tight.
6	5	and on

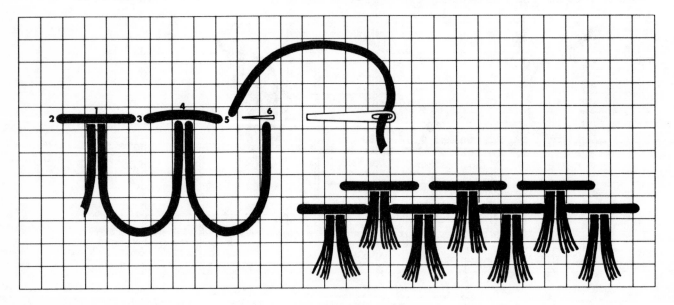

SURREY STITCH — one of the group of tufted stitches. It may be cut for a velvetlike surface or left with loops uncut for a harder, frieze-type surface. This stitch is best worked on penelope canvas. When using mono canvas, work over 2 threads as 1 to insure that the knots don't slip. Works fairly quickly after you've practiced a bit.

Work horizontal rows from left to right, *bottom to top* (so loops are not in the way of next row of stitches). Needle is worked twice into 1 mesh to complete each tuft.

Insert needle *from the front* at mesh 1 and come out at mesh 2 (diagram **a**). Holding down tag end with thumb, carry yarn up and insert needle at mesh 3 from *right to left* under the vertical double thread, bringing needle out in starting mesh 1 (diagram **b**). Pull stitch down tight (diagram **c**). Cut end to desired length (or leave uncut for a loop finish). Make next stitch working to right, beginning in mesh 3.

For next row start at left again, 2 or 3 meshes *above* last row, depending on how thick and full surface is to be. Trim evenly when area is finished.

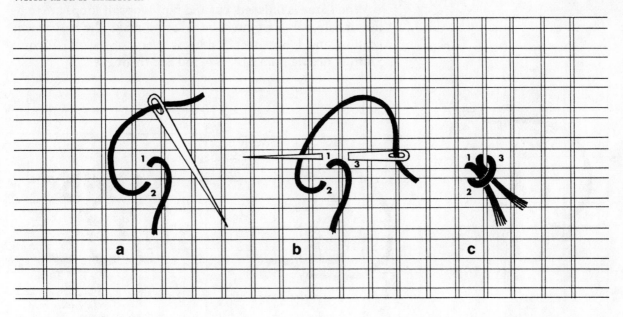

a   b   c

VELVET STITCH (Astrakhan stitch) — a pile stitch held firmly with a Cross stitch, worked over 1 double thread intersection on penelope canvas or 2 threads on mono canvas. It makes a finer (closer together) stitch when worked on penelope. The stitch will make a pile similar to that on Oriental rugs; the yarn must be thick and full to get the best effect. Works easily but slowly because it takes three thrusts of the needle to complete each stitch.

Work in horizontal rows from *left to right, bottom to top.* On mono canvas, working over 2 horizontal and vertical threads, bring needle up at left and put it in 2 meshes to the right, making a loop of yarn; hold it with thumb. Now bring needle up 2 meshes *below* start of stitch and make a slanted stitch up to the right over 2 threads (diagram **a**). Bring needle up in starting mesh again (diagram **b**) and make a slanted stitch *down* to right over 2 threads, completing the Cross stitch which holds the loop. Begin next stitch 2 meshes above last stitch (mesh 2). Complete row. Start next row at the left, 1 or 2 threads *above* last row.

When area is finished, cut and fluff loops. If loops are to be left uncut, extra care must be taken to make the loops even. Making the loops over a narrow piece of cardboard or a knitting needle is an easy way to keep them even.

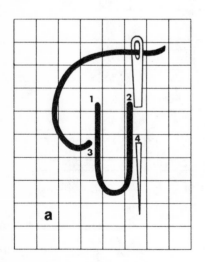 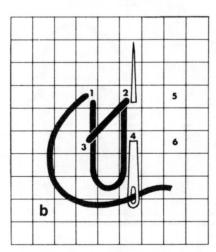 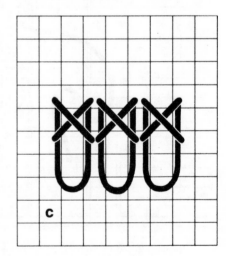

(end of Tufted Stitches)

VAN DYKE STITCH

Here is a decorative stitch for accenting, banding, or stripes. A small stitch, it will wear well. Works easily and fairly quickly.

Work vertical rows from *top to bottom,* right to left. Each stitch is worked over 3 horizontal and 2 vertical threads. Slant first stitch *up to right* over 3 horizontal and 2 vertical threads, bring needle out to left under 2 vertical threads and slant stitch *down to right* over 3 horizontal and 2 vertical threads. Now bring needle out 2 threads below start of first stitch. Slant stitch up to right over 3 horizontal and 2 vertical threads and continue making these overlapping stitches to end of row. Start next row at top, working to the left of the row just completed. This forms a tight, slightly raised braidlike rib.

Other counts can be used. For example, work down from the top over 6 (or 8) horizontal threads. An Upright Gobelin stitch can be used as a fill-in stitch between Van Dyke units. Try using yarn a shade lighter or darker, or use floss or perle cotton.

WEB STITCH

This stitch is used for filling or accent areas where a close, woven look is desired. This special-use stitch makes a hard-wearing surface, but it is slow to work up. It can be worked on mono or penelope canvas. On penelope the small "hold" stitches are worked between the double threads. The long diagonal stitches always start at the same side and the hold stitches are worked back over the long stitches and the canvas intersections.

On penelope: Start with a Tent stitch (1–2) at top left. Then bring needle up in mesh below starting stitch and slant a stitch up to the right over 2 intersections (3–4). This is your first "long" stitch. Bring needle up between the double threads under the Tent stitch at 5 (being careful not to split the yarn of the stitch) to make small stitch over the long stitch and into the double thread intersection diagonally opposite at 6. This is your first "hold" stitch. Now bring needle up in mesh below start of previous long stitch (7) and slant a long stitch up over 3 intersections (8). Bring needle up between double threads at intersection to left in position to make hold stitch (9–10). Complete next hold stitch (11–12). Continue laying slanted stitches up to right and working back over them with short hold stitches worked between the double threads. This is the English or Continental method and it is easy to work on a frame.

On mono: Start with a Tent stitch at top right. Then bring needle up 2 meshes below and slant a long stitch up to the left over 2 intersections (3–4). Bring needle up in mesh below and make a Tent stitch over long slanting stitch and thread intersection. Carry needle down under 2 horizontal threads (like working the Diagonal Tent or Basket Weave stitch, page 29) and make another Tent stitch over long stitch and 1 thread intersection. Bring needle up 2 meshes below and make a long slanting stitch up to left. Work back over it with Tent stitches. Continue in this manner until area is completed.

This stitch can be worked in other directions, too. For example, canvas can be given a quarter turn to right or left and stitches will slant in different directions. Patterns can also be worked out by making the hold stitches in an irregular count, giving texture to the surface. Also, a tweedy look can be achieved by working in two colors and/or textures of yarn.

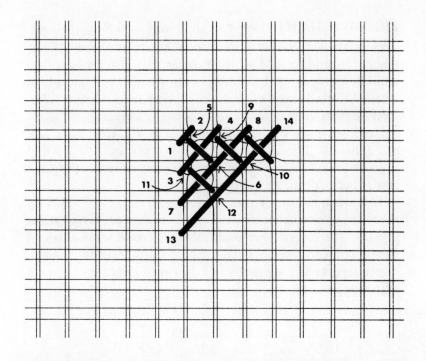

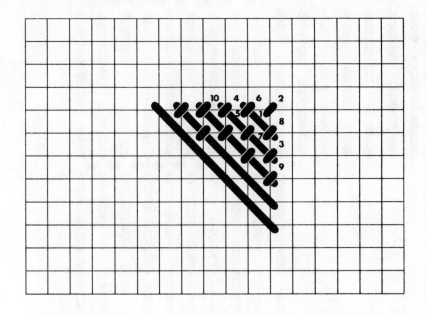

ZIGZAG STITCH (Princess stitch, Berlin Border stitch)

This is an old, basically decorative stitch used for stripes, edging, grounding, and accent textures. (See also Reverse Pyramid Border, page 171.) Will wear quite well if pattern is kept small. Most effective in several colors or tones of one color. Don't pull stitches tight. Covers canvas quickly.

First, work rows of straight stitches over 2, then 3, 4, 5, 4, and 3 threads. The second row is worked to mesh into the first row, or it may be placed with its straight edge abutting the straight edge of the first row.

This stitch has many variations. The pyramid units may be made larger or smaller by working over more or fewer canvas threads. The rows of pyramids may be separated by a row of Tent stitch, Cross stitch, Back stitch, or Upright Gobelin stitch. These accent rows are pretty in a darker or brighter yarn or in a floss or perle cotton.

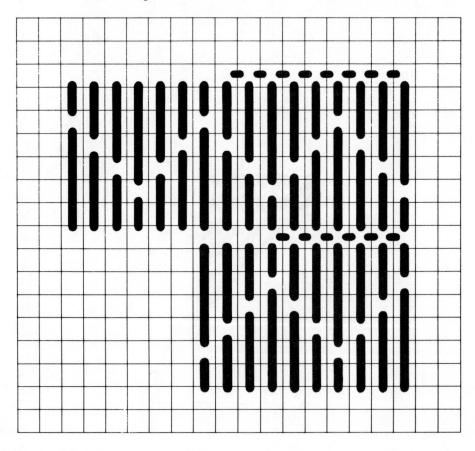

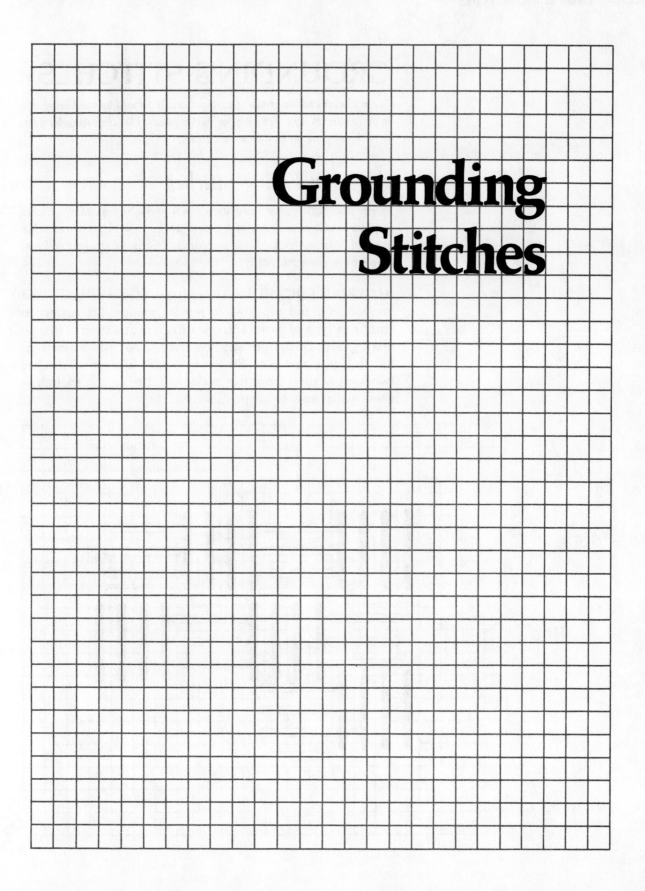

Grounding Stitches

GROUNDING STITCHES

An almost endless group of patterns can be formed by combining two or more stitches for large areas or backgrounds. Use the examples here, or make up your own of favorite stitches.

Algerian Filling Stitches

The first five stitches below are from a group of grounding stitches inspired by old embroidery and woven fabrics from Algeria and other areas of North Africa. These patterns use Satin or straight stitches, arranged in geometric patterns.

ALGERIAN SQUARES — Satin stitches placed vertically and horizontally, and repeated in regular groups. It's easiest to work this type of pattern in one direction at a time — that is, work groups of upright stitches first (working in rows from left to right), and then fill in areas with horizontal stitches (working in rows from the top down). Be careful, though — check your count to keep units even.

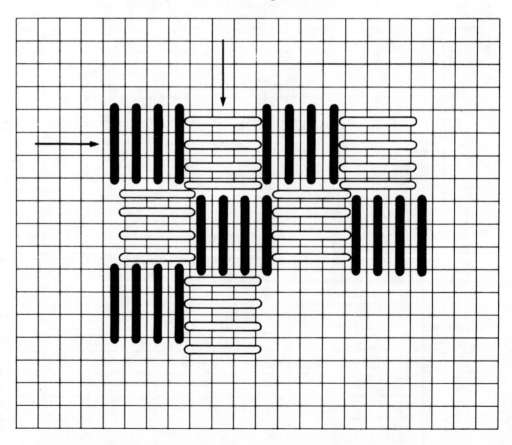

ALGERIAN STRIPE — upright Satin stitches repeated in regular groups. Yarn should be full enough to cover canvas completely. Good in one or two colors.

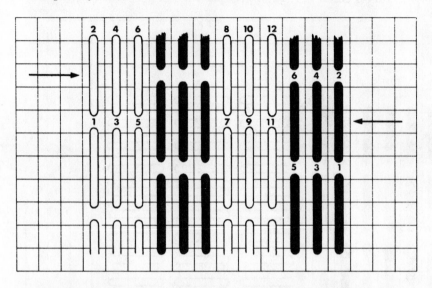

BAMBOO — long and short upright stitches are separated by horizontal stitches. Work in horizontal rows over and back, alternating three short stitches, then three long stitches over area. The horizontal divider stitches work most easily in a separate journey, making diagonal rows from the top down.

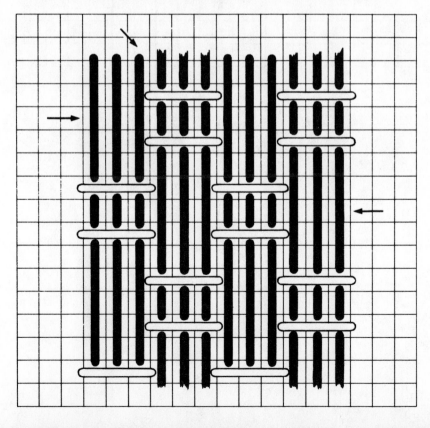

CHECKERBOARD — like Algerian Squares, this pattern is made up of Satin stitches, placed vertically and horizontally, and repeated in regular groups.

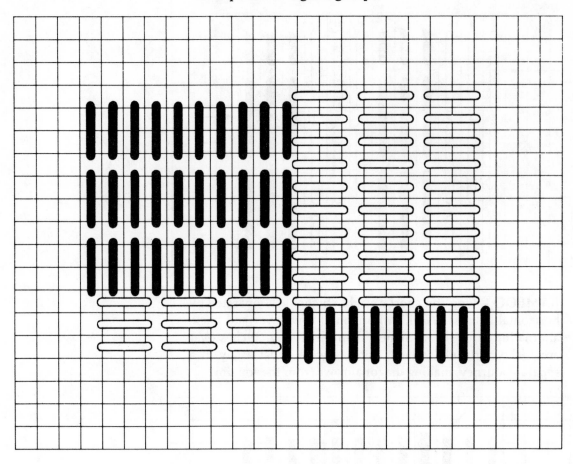

VICTORIAN GROUND — similar to Algerian Stripe, except here the groups are divided by a horizontal stitch. Good in one color for an allover design. Two or three colors can be worked into stripes, checks, or plaids.

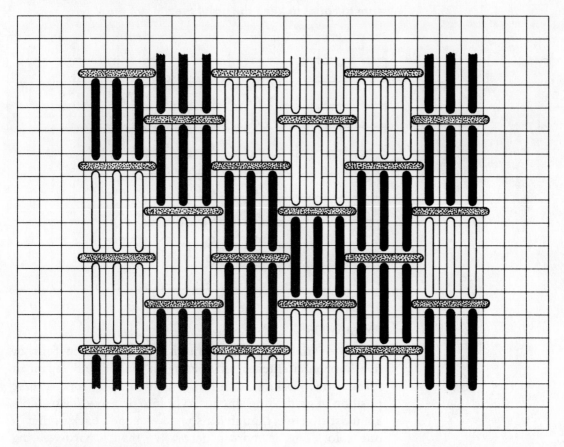

(end of Algerian Filling Stitches)

HALF AND HALF

This combines Scotch and Tent stitches in one square unit. Also try it with Scotch stitch and Reverse Tent stitch (see Continental Herringbone stitch, page 92). Pretty in one or two colors.

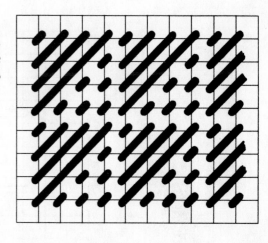

KALEM SQUARED

Blocks of Kalem stitch are worked in two colors, or alternating blocks of Kalem stitch and Reverse Tent stitch (see Continental Herringbone stitch, page 92) are made for variation. Be sure to count to keep the units even.

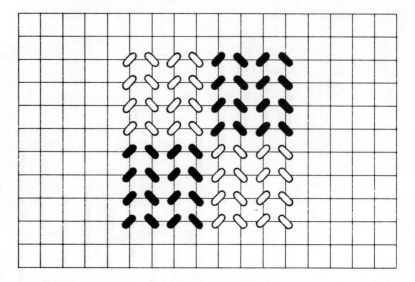

PYRAMIDS

This is a variation of the Milanese stitch. Use three, four, or five horizontal stitches, graduating in length, and repeat to form a row, working from top to bottom. Next row, reverse position of graduating stitches to fit into first row. Two colors are most effective, though it also makes a good background in one color. This is more a decorative than a hard-wearing stitch. Variations may be worked out by doubling stitches in each size.

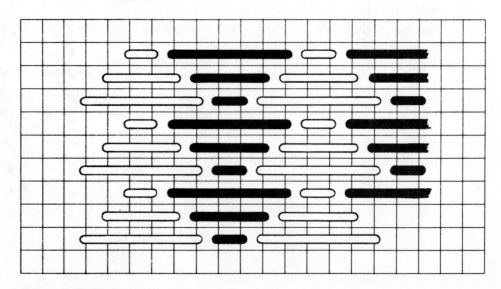

ROSEMARY

This is an old grounding stitch composed of Tent stitch squares separated by double upright and horizontal stitches, with a Cross stitch joining the straight stitches.

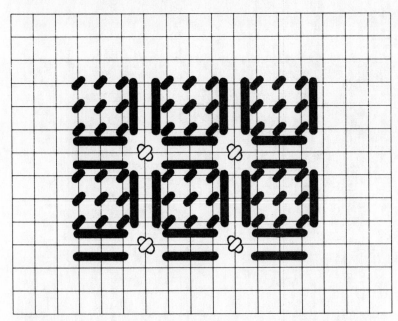

Variation: Try using Scotch stitch squares divided by the straight stitches. One, two, or three colors may be used.

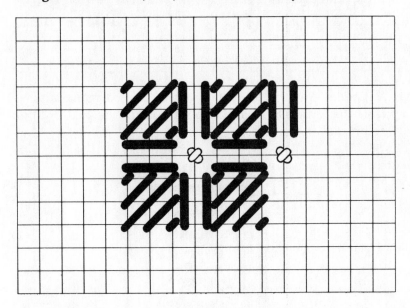

SATIN SQUARES

Here, square motifs worked with three or four graduated Satin stitches have a French Knot or Cross stitch for the center. Each square motif may be outlined with Tent stitch.

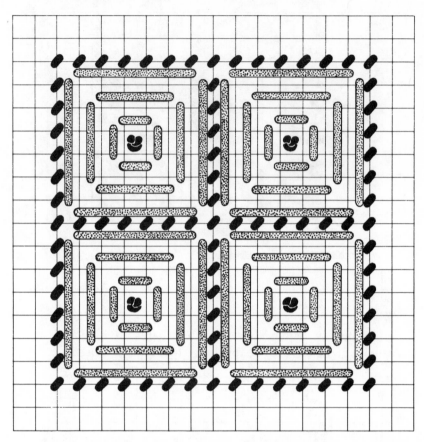

Variation: Work *into* an eyelet stitch by using diagonal stitches from the corners to the center of each unit. One, two, or three colors may be used.

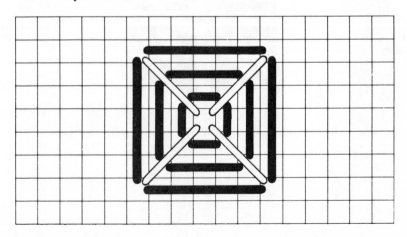

SMYRNA CROSS AND SCOTCH STITCH

Alternate stitches and rows for a pretty, patterned ground. For another look, alternate Smyrna and Star stitches in one or two colors.

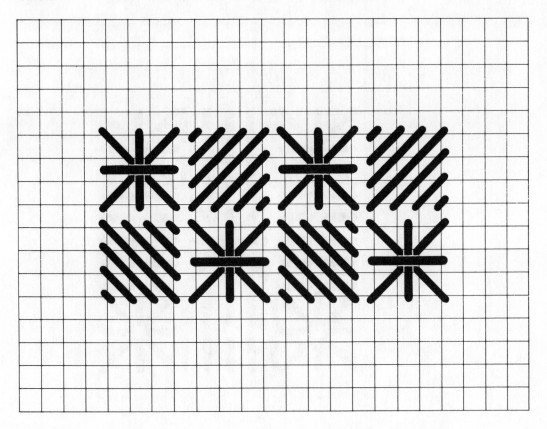

STAR AND GOBELIN

This is a pretty grounding made up of alternating Star and Straight Gobelin stitches, worked upright and horizontally. Two tones of one color or two colors are good.

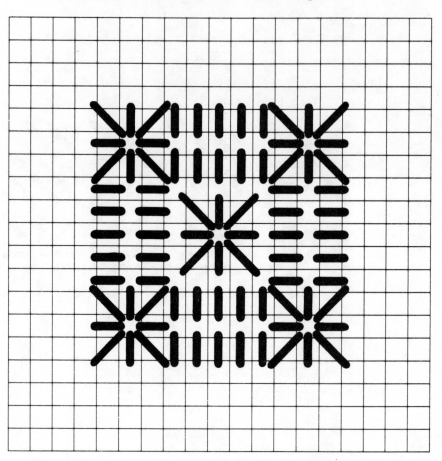

Border Stitches

BORDER STITCHES

Pretty borders can be worked by using one or several rows of various unit stitches such as Eye, Scotch, or the Leviathans, or alternating stitches such as Gobelin, Tent, and Scotch stitches in endless variations. More complicated borders using general stitches are illustrated here. Care must always be taken to make borders even. Count each side carefully so the correct number of threads is reserved. For example, a border requiring a count of 4 threads for each stitch must have a total number of threads divisible by 4. Corners may be squared off and a motif stitch used, or they may be mitered. To miter on the canvas, draw a light diagonal line at each corner and work the design just to the line. Or work out design on graph paper; then fold the paper on the diagonal to form the miter (or turning) line.

ALGERIAN BORDER

Worked over 12 threads, this border combines Straight Gobelin, Satin (horizontally), Back, and Cross stitches. It is prettiest when worked in two, three, or four colors.

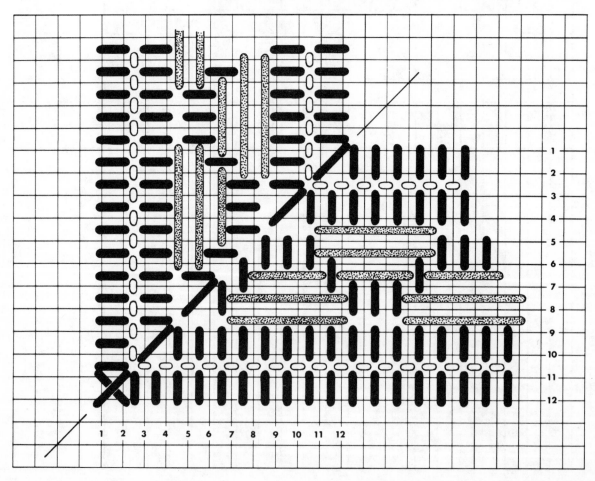

GOBELIN AND CROSS

Combining these stitches makes a pretty border, but it takes a bit of thought to keep the slant of the stitches going in the correct direction. Combining Slanting Gobelin stitch, Cross stitch, and Tent stitch, it is worked over 14 threads. Try two or three colors.

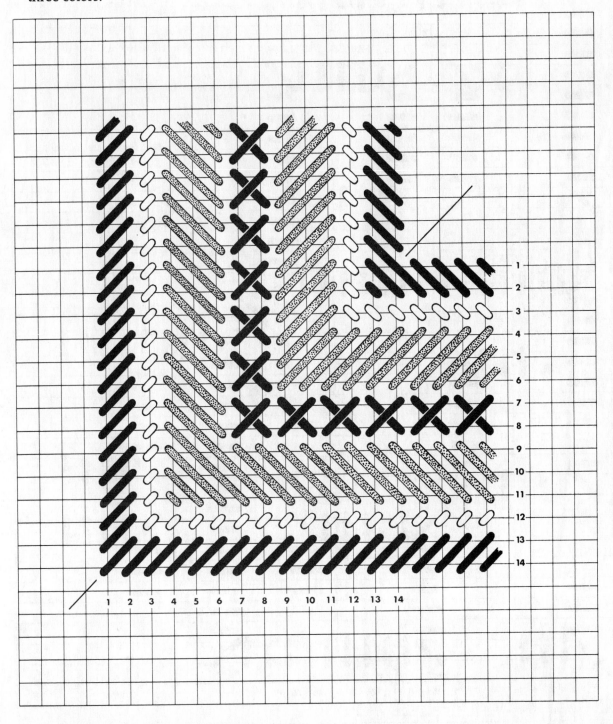

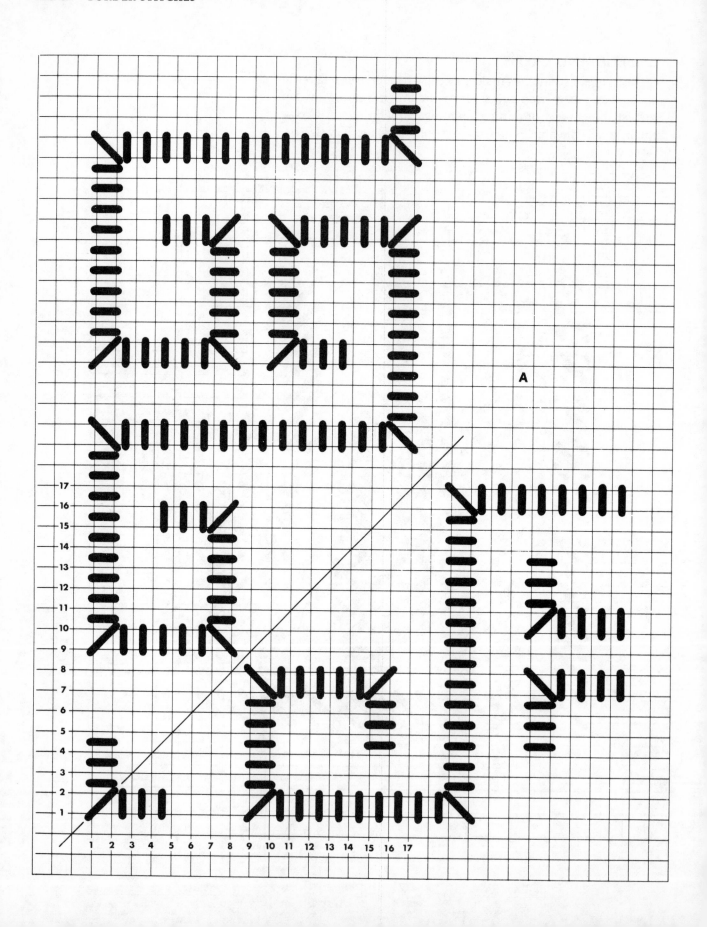

GREEK KEY BORDER

There are many variations of this classic, and in all the stitches *must* be counted. A is worked over 17 threads in Straight Gobelin stitch with a slanted stitch at each corner (or it may be worked in Tent stitch). B — a continuously alternating "T" border — may be worked in Tent stitch or Straight Gobelin stitch. These borders can be scaled to almost any count to fit the area. Work the border, and then work the background.

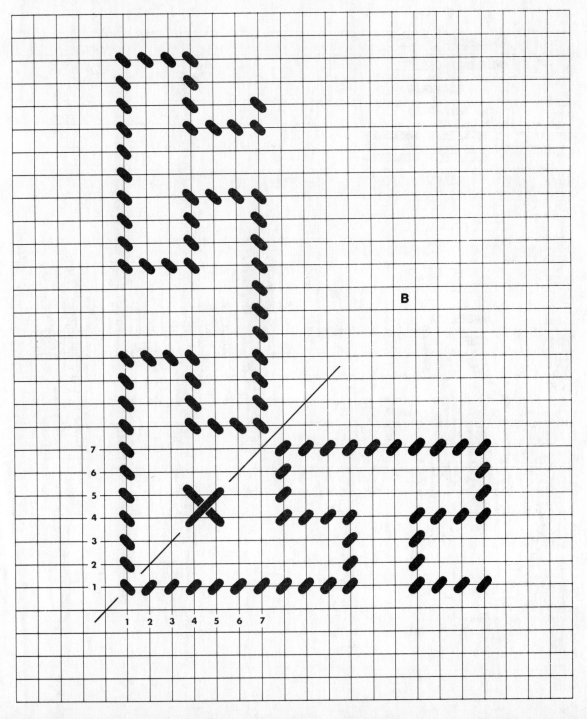

IRREGULAR GOBELIN BAND

This is an open border in Upright Gobelin stitch, grounded with Tent stitch. Work over 7 threads. Try this in one or three colors. Count the area carefully. Work the border and then work the background.

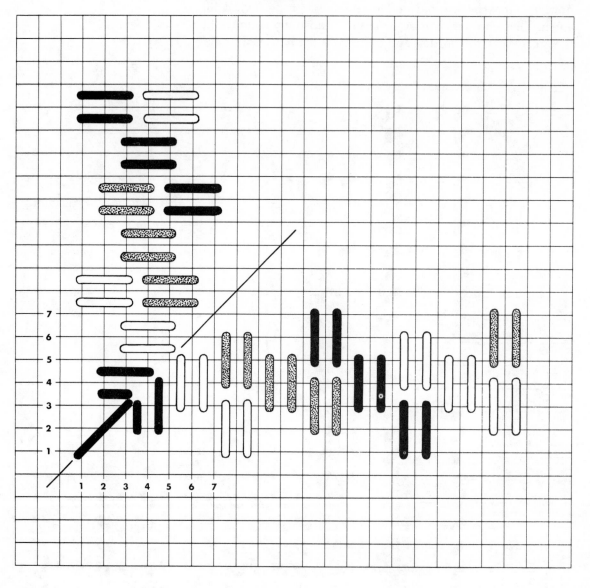

REVERSE PYRAMID BORDER (Princess Border)

An effective, easy-to-do border of straight and cross stitches, this is worked over 14 threads in one, two, or three colors. If border is not mitered, Triangle stitch (page 145) can be fitted into the corner for a finishing motif. Count and mark area for border. Work pyramid rows first and then fill in with Upright Gobelin stitch rows.

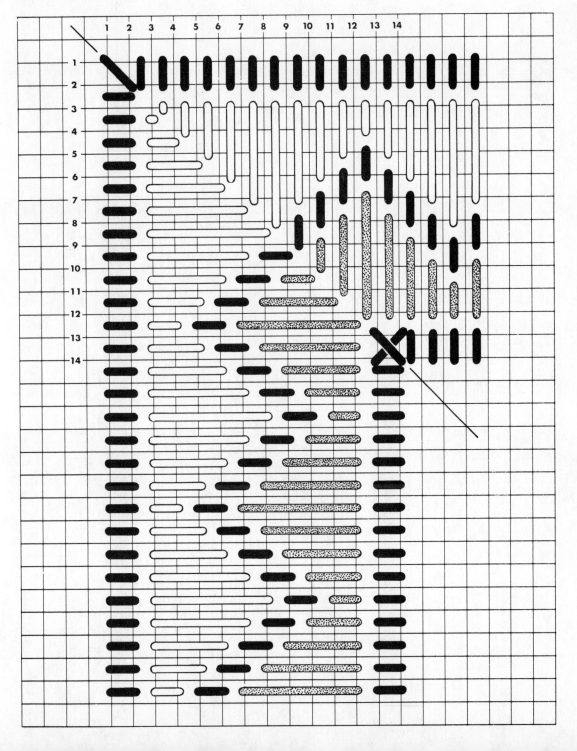

Know-How
Notes

KNOW-HOW NOTES

The canvas should usually be worked so that the selvage is at the side of the needlepoint piece; this is a *must* with penelope. At least 1½ inches of *unworked* canvas should be left all around every piece of needlepoint to allow for blocking and finishing.

FULLNESS OF YARN

To cover canvas evenly, yarn should be just thick enough. Try the yarn on the canvas you've selected—some stitches require more or fewer plies for best results. *As a guide:* For the basic Tent stitch on 10 count canvas, use one full strand of 3-ply Persian yarn or one full strand of 4-ply tapestry yarn. On 12 or 14 count canvas, split 3-ply Persian yarn and use 2 plies in the needle; on 18 count canvas, use 1 ply. For a fuller yarn for larger canvases (8 or 5 count), use two or three full strands of Persian or tapestry yarn.

PULLING OF CANVAS

Canvas will often pull out of shape while it is being worked. This is because of the slant of the stitches and usually is not permanent. When the needlepoint is finished, it should be blocked (stretched and straightened) to its original size and shape.

USING A FRAME

Needlepoint that has been worked on a frame will not be as out of shape when finished as a canvas worked in-the-hand, although it too should be blocked when completed to even the surface and close and fluff the stitches.

If you choose to work with a frame, select a tapestry or rug frame—*do not* use an embroidery hoop for canvas work—or make a frame easily and inexpensively with artists' stretchers, wooden strips 1½ inches wide that are slotted at each end to lock together. (Stretchers of various lengths are available at art supply stores and some art needlework shops.) A large frame is most versatile because smaller canvases can be "tied in" to it by lacing with heavy thread or string.

If you choose a roller frame when doing a large piece, be careful to "relax" the rollers so the canvas is not held taut during periods when you're not working on it. It's possible that the needlepoint will stretch if it is held taut on the frame for an extended length of time.

When using a frame, it is best to work with one hand on top and the other under the frame. Put the needle in with the hand on top; pull the needle through and return it to the top with the hand under the frame. After a little practice, this method becomes quick and easy, and gives your stitches a firm, even tension.

TENSION

All stitches, basic or fancy, should be worked with even tension. *Working too loosely* will cause the yarn to "crowd" the canvas meshes, making the unworked canvas threads push together. *Working too tightly* will pull canvas threads together, causing the canvas or spaces to show between stitches, and the canvas will pull out of shape more than usual.

STITCH METHOD

Many stitches can be worked in several ways. The methods diagrammed in this book are those found easiest to do, and/or those that give the fullest or most even coverage on both the front and back of the canvas.

STARTING AND FASTENING OFF YARN

Experienced embroiderers and needleworkers have always been concerned with the neat appearance of the reverse side of their work. For canvas work, *never* use a knot at the back for beginning a strand of yarn. Instead, begin or fasten off yarn by running the needle under worked stitches for about 1 inch, pull the yarn end through, and clip it off. (Always clip off the tag end as you finish each strand of yarn; don't let tag ends hang loose.) Don't anchor ends in another color, but run the end back through the stitches just finished. (Reason: A dark yarn run through a lighter tone may show, making the section look soiled; a light color run through a darker shade may make the area appear "dusty" or grayed.) When running an end through stitches, *always* run the yarn through *with the grain* of the canvas; the yarn will lie smoother and not pull the stitches so much. *Never* run yarn through stitches in a diagonal direction (even in the Basket Weave stitch); this is likely to make a fine ridge on the surface that may show even after blocking.

WASTE KNOTS

A waste knot may be used for starting a first needleful of yarn.

Knot the end of the yarn and insert the needle *from the front* of the canvas (knot is on face of canvas) about 1 inch diagonally below the first stitch. Bring the needle up in position for your first stitch and work along, working *over* the end held by the knot. When the work has progressed as far as the knot, clip the knot off, and continue working.

ON THE BACK
Stitches on the back of the canvas should be even, regular, and smooth. Many needlepointers take pride, as experienced embroiderers do, in seeing that the back of their work is as neat and attractive as the front. Of course, some stitches work up so the back is more even than others—but a change of direction, untidy finishing off of tag ends, and helter-skelter carrying of yarn across areas all make for a messy reverse side of the canvas and should be avoided.

UNUSUAL STITCHES
Don't get "carried away" with a pretty or fun-to-do stitch. Always consider your finished piece and its use—for example, not all stitches are adaptable for hard wear. If you are not sure, check the Detail List and/or work a sample to double-check. Remember: The longer or looser the stitch, the less wear it will give, and the more it may snag.

FILL-IN STITCHES
When working pattern stitches, it is necessary to fill in at the edges and around a design area with smaller stitches. You can sometimes use a part of the pattern stitch unit for these purposes, or small compensating stitches.

SMOOTH STITCHES
Yarn of 2 or more plies should lie smoothly on the surface as the yarn is pulled through the canvas. A counterclockwise turn of the needle between thumb and first finger between every second or third stitch will help. With many stitches you can guide the lay of the yarn with your left thumb as you pull it through the canvas.

OVER-STITCHING
An effective method for accent, detailing, or texture is over-stitching. By using selected variety stitches or embroidery

(crewel) stitches *on top of* the finished needlepoint, interesting new effects can be achieved. These stitches may be worked in the same or a contrasting color in wool or in other yarns such as silk or cotton floss, string, metallic thread, and so forth.

WORKING BORDERS

Because many border designs are worked on a stitch count, it is usually best to count the threads (sides, top, and bottom) and mark the section so it contains a total number of threads that is a multiple of the threads used for the stitch unit. These border sections should be marked *before* the background is worked, although the border usually isn't worked until after the background has been stitched. Generally, it is best to start working at the center of a border area, working first to the left, then picking up the design at the center again and working to the right. This assures that the pattern will be even from end to end.

BEADS AND FOUND OBJECTS

Combining small beads with Tent stitch was popular in the late nineteenth century. Today, innumerable objects—beads in all sizes and all materials (glass, wood, metal, etc.), shells, sequins, tiny decorative mirrors, even "found" objects—can be worked into a design or over-stitched on a design to create special textures, for accent and design effects, and for color. Try it, it's fun!

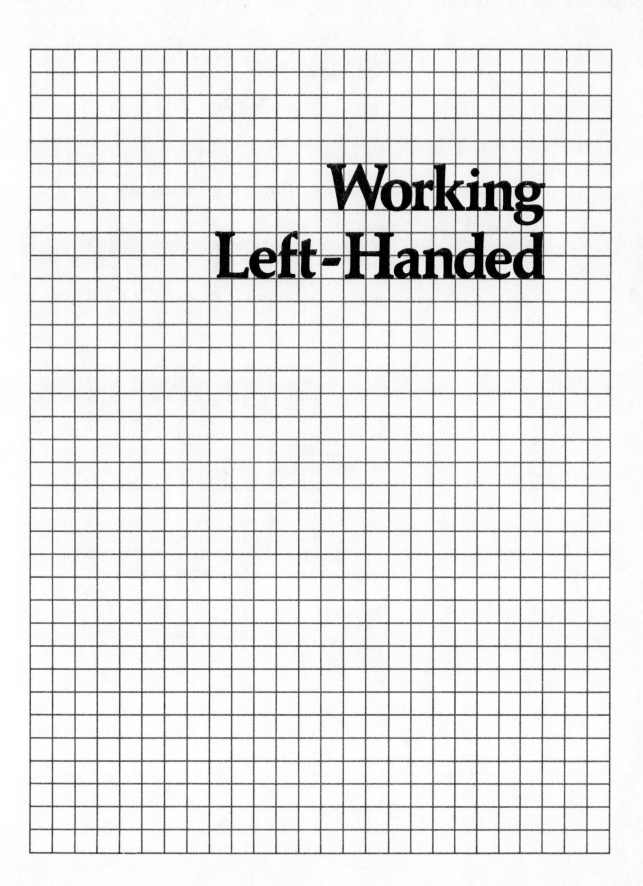

Working
Left-Handed

WORKING LEFT-HANDED

One of the challenges in giving instructions for needlepoint is to explain it so that everyone, whether working right-handed or left-handed, can complete stitches with the traditional look. This means, for the Tent stitch and other slanted stitches, that the stitch must slant upward *from left to right* on the front of the canvas.

Most needlepoint instructions, including those in this book, are given for right-handed needleworkers. Often the directions written for southpaws are unsatisfactory because they usually reverse the slant of the stitches—that is, Tent stitch, Basket Weave stitch, Mosaic stitch, and other slanted stitches are worked so that the stitches slant from right to left instead of from left to right. Only a few stitches, such as upright stitches and eyelet stitches, are done as easily left-handed as right-handed from general instructions.

Here's a simple solution that will allow the left-handed needleworker to use the instructions in this book to create needlepoint with the traditional look.

When you're ready to begin, give the canvas a quarter turn to the *right*. The design will be on its side, with the top toward your right hand (see illustration). Always hold the needlepoint canvas in this position for working.

Now, turn the instruction diagram a quarter turn to the *left*. Then just follow the general instructions and diagram. When the needlepoint is completed, the stitches will slant upward from left to right on the front of the canvas.

NEEDLEPOINT CANVAS

Top

right-handers
start here
▼

a quarter turn to the right ⟶

left-handers
start here
►

Top

STITCH DIAGRAM

a quarter turn to the left ⟵

Top

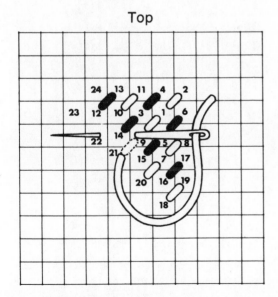

Working right-handed

Top

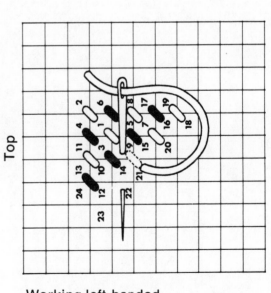

Working left-handed

Glossary

Background—the area surrounding motifs and/or the central design, extending to the outer edges of the area to be worked. (Also called grounding.) In pieces with the center design already worked, the needlepointer works *only* the background.

Blocking—reshaping the needlepoint canvas to its original size and shape after the stitching is finished and all ends have been anchored and clipped.

Canvas—woven cotton (or linen) fabric on which needlepoint embroidery is worked. Usually it is heavily sized to help keep the threads even, and to give strength and firmness for working. There are two basic types of needlepoint canvas. *Mono canvas* is a single thread canvas made in an even, open weave; it is very easy to work on. The threads cross each other in an over-under weave, with 1 horizontal thread and 1 vertical thread forming each intersection. (On *interlocking* or *leno canvas*, another kind of mono canvas, the single threads are 2-ply and locked together; they cannot be separated.) The best quality mono canvas has a highly polished finish, not a dull or pasty surface. It is usually white, though some kinds are ecru or yellow. Mono canvas is available in different widths and a range of mesh sizes. The size of the canvas is indicated by the number of threads to the running inch. *Penelope canvas,* also called double thread or duo canvas, is woven with 2 vertical threads and 2 horizontal threads forming each intersection. It is usually ecru in color, although white and yellow are also available. The sizes most often used are: 5 mesh (or rug) canvas, and 10 and 12 mesh canvas, usually used for working Petit Point and regular needlepoint on the same piece.

Count—a term used to indicate the number of threads to the running inch in giving the size of a canvas. For instance, 10 count canvas has 10 threads to the inch. (The term *mesh* is sometimes used for this pupose: 10 mesh canvas also has 10 threads to the inch.)

Compensating stitches—when working pattern stitches, it is necessary to fill in at the edges and around a design area with smaller stitches. These small stitches are usually Tent stitch or Reverse Tent stitch (see Continental Herringbone stitch, page 92). They cover sections where the pattern falls short of the area, where the pattern stitch must be shortened to fit the area, or to square a corner. These small stitches are also called fill-in stitches.

Embroidery—the art of ornamenting a plain fabric by working designs with a needle and one or more kinds of yarn, often in many colors.

Encroach—to overlap the preceding row by 1 or 2 threads. (When stitches are worked into the *same* mesh, they share the mesh rather than encroach.)

Fill-in stitches—see **Compensating stitches**

Filling—the design area, or any smaller area within the design area; not the background.

Filling threads—the crosswise threads in a woven fabric (canvas). Referred to in stitch descriptions as *horizontal threads*.

Floats—long stitches made by the yarn lying over several canvas threads.

Frame—a lightweight wooden support, often on an adjustable floor stand, used to hold canvas taut and firm for working on it. Frames should be rectangular or square; embroidery *hoops*, which are round or oval, should *not* be used for canvas work. Frames are available in several styles and sizes.

Graph paper—drafting paper ruled with evenly spaced horizontal and vertical lines that form evenly spaced squares. For use in working out designs for needlepoint, each square represents one Tent stitch. Graph paper is available in a number of sizes, but the 10-squares-to-1-inch size is most useful for needlepoint.

Gros point—needlepoint worked in Tent stitch or Cross stitch on mono or penelope canvas that has 8 to 12 threads to the inch.

Grounding—see **Background**

Held-down thread—on mono canvas, a vertical or horizontal thread *over* which another thread passes (as viewed from the front of the canvas). See the diagram of mono canvas on page 23, as well as the accompanying text and note, to understand how the term is used in this book.

Horizontal threads—see **Filling threads**

Interlocking canvas—see **Canvas**

Journey—the term used to indicate working across one row of needlepoint. Some stitches require working over each row (or the canvas area) two or three times to complete the stitch. Thus a stitch may take three journeys to complete.

Mesh—in needlepoint, the opening or hole between intersecting canvas threads.

Mono canvas—see **Canvas**

Motif—the central design of a needlepoint pattern, or a small pattern or stitch used singly or in groups to form a design.

Needlepoint—canvas-work embroidery, usually employing wool yarn on open-mesh canvas. (The term is also used to refer to the stitch most frequently used: Tent stitch.) Generally, needlepoint is a colorful and decorative fabric that is very durable—suitable for rugs, upholstery, handbags, and so forth. Variations in types of yarn, stitches, and canvas may produce a more decorative but less durable needlepoint.

Over-stitch—to stitch on top of finished needlepoint. Over-stitching can be used to outline, or to give accent, texture, or dimensional bulk to an area.

Penelope canvas—see **Canvas**

Persian yarn—a 3-ply wool yarn usually sold by the ounce. Persian yarn can be used full strand (3-ply) or divided into 1 or 2 plies as required for the canvas size and stitch. Persian yarn is fine quality, wears well, works up evenly, and is available in hundreds of colors.

Petit Point—needlepoint worked in Tent stitch on fine mono or penelope canvas, usually 18, 22, 24, or more threads to the inch. On penelope canvas the double threads must be separated and a stitch worked over each intersection.

Pile—closely worked loop stitches, which may be cut or left as loops, that form a deep, springy surface. Also see **Tufting**.

Ply—a single strand of yarn. Two- or 3-ply yarns are made by twisting together two or three single yarns. Persian yarn is 3-ply; tapestry yarn is usually 4-ply.

Quick Point—needlepoint worked on large-mesh (rug) canvas, usually 5 threads to the inch, with rug yarn or with three full strands of Persian or tapestry yarn.

Rug canvas—a double thread (penelope) large-mesh canvas, usually with 3½, 5, or 7 threads to the inch. Used for Quick Point.

Sampler—a piece of needlework made to learn or practice a variety of stitches.

Selvage—the closely woven lengthwise edge of a woven fabric, finished so as to prevent raveling.

Sizing—a finishing process used on yarns or fabrics to give added strength, stiffness, and smoothness.

Tapestry needle—a special needle, used on needlepoint canvas, that has a blunt point and an elongated eye for easy threading of wool yarn. Generally, sizes 18 to 20 are best for needlepoint—size 18 for 10 mesh canvas, size 20 for finer yarns and 14 mesh canvas. Size 22 is usually used for Petit Point.

Tapestry yarn—a soft, tightly twisted 4-ply wool yarn usually sold in 40-yard skeins. It is the correct size for working Tent stitch on 10 mesh canvas. Tapestry yarn can be split for Petit Point, though it does not split as easily as Persian yarn. A variety of colors is available.

Tension—the amount of strength, or pull, put on the yarn to make each stitch. Even tension should be maintained to make the smoothest and most even needlework.

Tent stitch—the primary needlepoint stitch. It is a small, short stitch worked over 1 thread intersection on mono canvas or 1 double thread intersection on penelope canvas. Tent stitch may be worked by different methods, but it is *always* slanted from left to right on the front of the canvas.

Thread—any strand, single or multi-ply, of cotton, silk, wool, synthetic, or metallic yarn used for embroidery and canvas work. As used in this book, the word *threads* refers to the vertical (warp) and horizontal (filling) threads of the needlepoint canvas; the term *yarn* or *wool* is used to refer to the embroidering yarn. For regular needlepoint on penelope canvas, each pair of double canvas threads is usually referred to as 1 thread.

Tramé/Trammed—in Tramé work, long stitches are laid along the threads of the canvas and then worked over in any of several stitches—usually Tent stitch or Gobelin stitch—to make the stitch appear fuller, to give depth of color, for decorative effect, for grounding, or to fill small areas. Tramé may refer to the method of stitching (a stitch may be trammed) *or* to the yarn that is laid in on the canvas.

Tufting—a method of needlework where stitches made with a soft, full yarn are looped and knotted into the canvas to form a thick, dense surface. There are two ways to finish tufted work: The loops may be left as loops, or the loops may be cut and the ends fluffed to make a soft, fuzzy surface. Also see **Pile**.

Vertical threads—see **Warp**

Warp—the lengthwise threads in a woven fabric (canvas). Referred to in stitch directions as *vertical threads*.

Waste knot—a knot in the end of the yarn put in from the *front* of the canvas and later cut off, used to hold a tag end of yarn when it cannot be fastened under already worked stitches, as when starting a first needleful of yarn.

Yarn—a strand made by twisting together natural and/or synthetic fibers to form a long continuous thread. Two or more of these strands are twisted together to make a ply yarn. Yarn used for needlepoint is usually 100 percent wool, made of long staple fibers with a medium-hard twist to give strength to the yarn so it will wear well and can be pulled through the canvas without roughing up. Also see **Persian yarn** and **Tapestry yarn**.

Bibliography

Ambuter, Carolyn, *Carolyn Ambuter's Complete Book of Needlepoint.* New York: Thomas Y. Crowell Co., 1972.

de Dillmont, Therese, *Encyclopedia of Needlework.* D.M.C. Library. Mulhouse, France.

Hanley, Hope, *Needlepoint.* Rev. ed. New York: Charles Scribner's Sons, 1975.

Hanley, Hope, *Needlepoint in America.* New York: Charles Scribner's Sons, 1969.

Harbeson, Georgiana Brown, *American Needlework.* Bonanza Books. New York: Coward, McCann and Geoghegan, Inc., 1938.

Lantz, Sherlee, *A Pageant of Pattern for Needlepoint Canvas.* 2nd ed. New York: Grosset and Dunlap, Inc., 1975.

Matthews, Sibyl I., *Needle-made Rugs.* Great Neck, New York: Hearthside Press, Inc., 1960.

Rhodes, Mary, *Needlepoint: The Art of Canvas Embroidery.* London: Octopus Books Ltd., 1974.

Schiffer, Margaret B., *Historical Needlework of Pennsylvania.* New York: Charles Scribner's Sons, 1968.

Sidney, Sylvia, *Sylvia Sidney Needlepoint Book.* New York: Van Nostrand Reinhold Co., 1968.

Snook, Barbara, *Craft of Florentine Embroidery.* New York: Charles Scribner's Sons, 1967.

Snook, Barbara, *Needlework Stitches.* New York: Crown Publishers, Inc., 1963.

Springall, Diana, *Canvas Embroidery.* Newton Centre, Mass.: Charles T. Branford Company, 1969.

Thomas, Mary, *Mary Thomas's Dictionary of Embroidery Stitches.* London: Hadder and Staughton, 1934.

Williams, Elsa S., *Bargello: Florentine Canvas Work.* New York: Van Nostrand Reinhold Co., 1974.

Williams, Elsa S., *Creative Canvas Work.* New York: Van Nostrand Reinhold Co., 1975.

Wilson, Erica, *Needleplay.* New York: Charles Scribner's Sons, 1975.

Index
to Stitches